T0116215

Scott Thornbury's 101 Grammar Questions

Cambridge Handbooks for Language Teachers

This series, now with over 50 titles, offers practical ideas, techniques and activities for the teaching of English and other languages, providing inspiration for both teachers and trainers.

The Pocket Editions come in a handy, pocket-sized format and are crammed full of tips and ideas from experienced English language teaching professionals, to enrich your teaching practice.

Recent titles in this series:

Recent Pocket Editions:

Scott Thornbury's 101 Grammar Questions

Scott Thornbury

Consultant and editor: Anne O'Keeffe

CAMBRIDGE
UNIVERSITY PRESS

CAMBRIDGE
UNIVERSITY PRESS

University Printing House, Cambridge CB2 8BS, United Kingdom

One Liberty Plaza, 20th Floor, New York, NY 10006, USA

477 Williamstown Road, Port Melbourne, VIC 3207, Australia

314-321, 3rd Floor, Plot 3, Splendor Forum, Jasola District Centre, New Delhi - 110025, India

79 Anson Road, #06-04/06, Singapore 079906

Cambridge University Press is part of the University of Cambridge.

It furthers the University's mission by disseminating knowledge in the pursuit of
education, learning and research at the highest international levels of excellence.

www.cambridge.org
Information on this title: www.cambridge.org/9781108701457

© Cambridge University Press 2019

This publication is in copyright. Subject to statutory exception
and to the provisions of relevant collective licensing agreements,
no reproduction of any part may take place without the written
permission of Cambridge University Press.

First published 2019

20 19 18 17 16 15 14 13 12 11 10 9 8 7 6 5 4 3 2 1

A catalogue record for this publication is available from the British Library

ISBN   978-1-108-70145-7   Paperback
ISBN   978-1-108-70149-5   Apple iBook
ISBN   978-1-108-70151-8   Google ebook
ISBN   978-1-108-70150-1   Kindle ebook
ISBN   978-1-108-70148-8   eBooks.com ebook

Cambridge University Press has no responsibility for the persistence or accuracy
of URLs for external or third-party internet websites referred to in this publication,
and does not guarantee that any content on such websites is, or will remain,
accurate or appropriate. Information regarding prices, travel timetables, and other
factual information given in this work is correct at the time of first printing but
Cambridge University Press does not guarantee the accuracy of such information
thereafter.

Contents

G: Miscellaneous 101

Glossary 109

Index 114

Acknowledgements

The authors and publishers acknowledge the following sources of copyright material and are grateful for the permissions granted. While every effort has been made, it has not always been possible to identify the sources of all the material used, or to trace all copyright holders. If any omissions are brought to our notice, we will be happy to include the appropriate acknowledgements on reprinting and in the next update to the digital edition, as applicable.

Text

Question 9: Transport Trading Limited for the extract from 'London Underground Station'. Copyright © Transport for London. Reproduced with permission of Transport Trading Limited via Pulse Creative Ltd.

Corpus

Development of this publication has made use of the Cambridge English Corpus (CEC). The CEC is a multi-billion word computer database of contemporary spoken and written English. It includes British English, American English and other varieties of English. It also includes the Cambridge Learner Corpus, developed in collaboration with Cambridge English Language Assessment. Cambridge University Press has built up the CEC to provide evidence about language use that helps to produce better language teaching materials.

Cambridge Dictionaries

Cambridge dictionaries are the world's most widely used dictionaries for learners of English. The dictionaries are available in print and online at dictionary.cambridge.org. Copyright © Cambridge University Press, reproduced with permission.

Thanks

Thanks, once again, to my always encouraging publishing team, Karen Momber and Jo Timerick at Cambridge University Press, and to Alison Sharpe for her scrupulous but good-humoured editing. Special thanks to the consultant editor, Anne O'Keeffe, for her insight and guidance. And thanks to the many (mainly anonymous) teachers who responded to questionnaires and supplied many of the questions – I hope the answers won't disappoint!

Why I wrote this book

A glance at any website, discussion forum or social network shared by teachers of English suggests that teachers are constantly asking each other questions related to pedagogical grammar. These may simply be questions about terminology or categorization ('What's a clause?'; 'Is *like* a preposition?'), or they may seek to unravel subtle grammatical distinctions ('What's the difference between *for* and *since*?') or explain persistent learner errors ('Why is *She explained me it* wrong?'). Grammar reference books do not always satisfy the need for immediate answers, since these are seldom if ever organized according to the questions teachers ask, and often assume a degree of familiarity with terminology that many teachers do not have. (If you know the linguistic term you probably already know the answer!) This book is designed to fulfil this basic, everyday need, as well as being a book that I hope can be read for interest – and even pleasure – in its own right.

To choose the questions to include, I drew on my own experience as a teacher and teacher trainer and the many years I have spent talking to colleagues about language-related issues. I have also combed through social networks dedicated to language teaching, and have surveyed large numbers of teachers online. The resulting list does not claim to be exhaustive, but is intended to cover the main areas of pedagogical grammar that recur with some frequency in coursebooks, curricula and exams. Nor are the answers necessarily comprehensive: for the sake of clarity and brevity a lot of detail has had to be trimmed or left out altogether. But any serviceable pedagogical grammar reference should be able to fill in the gaps. This book aims to be a first port of call for teachers confronted by a grammar puzzle while planning lessons, reflecting on their teaching, grading assignments, or simply indulging a natural – and very professional – curiosity as to how language is structured and used.

For those readers wishing to follow up issues raised in the book, I would strongly recommend the following (and I hereby acknowledge my debt to their authors, while acknowledging that any errors in the text are mine alone):

Biber, D., Conrad, S. and Leech, G. (2002) *Longman Student Grammar of Spoken and Written English*. Harlow: Pearson Education.

Carter, R. and McCarthy, M. (2006) *Cambridge Grammar of English*. Cambridge: Cambridge University Press.

Collins COBUILD English Grammar (3rd edition: 2011). London: HarperCollins.

Cowan, R. (2008) *The Teacher's Grammar of English*. Cambridge: Cambridge University Press.

Downing, A. and Locke, P. (2005) *English Grammar: A University Course* (2nd edition). London: Routledge.

Swan, M. (2016) *Practical English Usage* (4th edition). Oxford: Oxford University Press.

For a textbook of tasks that explore English grammar for teaching purposes, I might suggest:

Thornbury, S. (2017) *About Language: Tasks for Teachers of English* (2nd edition). Cambridge: Cambridge University Press.

Note: Words in **bold** in the text are defined in the Glossary at the end. Invented examples that are marked with an asterisk (*) are non-grammatical; genuine examples of learners' errors are not so marked.

Also, all references to a corpus are (unless otherwise stated) to the Cambridge English Corpus, for access to which I am extremely grateful.

A: General questions about grammar

What counts as grammar? And how is grammar learned? These, and related, issues really need to be addressed before we look at specific areas of grammar. So in this section we address some of these big questions.

1   What counts as grammar?
2   Does English have a lot of grammar?
3   What is prescriptive grammar?
4   Are British and American grammars really different?
5   Is there a difference between written and spoken grammar?
6   Is grammar learned in a set order?
7   How is grammar best taught?
8   What is the point of rules?
9   Is there grammar beyond the sentence?
10 Is there a core grammar?

1　What counts as grammar?

What are we talking about when we talk about grammar?
For example, where does vocabulary end and grammar
start? Does grammar stop at the sentence?

grammar /ˈɡræməʳ/. *noun* **1** [U] (the study or use of) the rules about how words change their form and combine with words to make sentences. (*Cambridge Advanced Learners' Dictionary*, 2005)

Traditionally, the way 'words change their form' is called *morphology*. In English, this includes the way **verbs** change from the present to the past (*walk* → *walked*) or **nouns** change from singular to plural (*dog* → *dogs*). The way that words 'combine with words to make sentences' is called *syntax*. Thus, the order of words that can go before a noun (*both the two small black dogs*) is governed by rules of **syntax**, just as the way that this **phrase** forms part of a sentence: *Both the two small black dogs ran away*. Compare this with the ungrammatical: **The both two black small dogs away ran*.

So grammar deals with the morphology and syntax of sentences. But there are some problems. Morphology also describes the way that words change and combine to make other words: *bull + dog = bulldog; run + -er = runner; run + out + of = run out of*. Not to mention idioms like *go to the dogs, a dog's breakfast*. So there's a fuzzy line between vocabulary (i.e. what you might find in a dictionary) and grammar.

Also, grammar extends beyond sentences. Consider: *The dogs ran away. I chased them*. Here *them* refers back to *the dogs* in the previous sentence – suggesting that there's also some fuzziness between grammar and what is called *discourse* (see **9**).

Finally, a distinction needs to be made between grammar and usage: a sentence might be technically ungrammatical but commonly used, like *Long time no see*; or it may be grammatically feasible but highly unlikely, e.g. ?*The dogs had been being walked*.

Does English have a lot of grammar? **2**

It's a common perception that the success of English as a global language owes a lot to the fact that it has very little grammar. Is this true?

Anyone who has studied Spanish or Turkish will be aware that in these languages there are many different forms of the **verb**. Likewise, German and Russian have many different forms of the **noun**. English is much simpler in these respects. Regular verbs have four forms in all: *walk, walked, walks,* and *walking.* Most nouns have just two: *dog* and *dogs.* (Three if we count *dog's.*) This is because English is not a highly inflected language: it does not have a lot of grammatical endings.

But this doesn't mean that English is grammar-light. If that were the case, then English-speakers would be somewhat limited in terms of the meanings they could express. And English learners would only rarely make mistakes!

Despite being minimally inflected, verbs in English employ a variety of **auxiliaries** to express different shades of meaning: *I have walked, I had been walking,* etc., which, in combination with changes in word order, distinguish between statements and questions: *Did you walk? Has the dog been walked?* Likewise, English uses a wide variety of **determiners** to identify the reference of nouns: *a dog, those dogs, no dog, a great many of their dogs,* etc. As with **auxiliary verbs,** there are tight restrictions on the order of these function words. In fact, what English lacks in **inflections,** it makes up in terms of **syntax.** In the absence of case markings, the difference between *The dog bit the man* and *The man bit the dog* depends entirely on word order.

Nevertheless, for the purposes of communicating in English as an international language, it's arguable that learners only need a relatively small subset of the grammatical potential of English. This is the argument that inspired the development of Basic English in the 1930s, and, more recently, Globish, both of which claim to have streamlined the grammar of English.

3 | What is prescriptive grammar?

> A doctor's prescription tells you what medicine you should take. In similar fashion, a prescriptive grammar tells you what you should say or write.

Most people associate *grammar* with the kinds of rules they were taught at school in classes called either English, or Language Arts. These are typically rules of 'correct usage' or 'good style'. They are invariably associated with educated or even prestigious varieties of the language, as opposed to colloquial language or, worse, slang. For example:

- Do not say: *You are taller than me*. Say: *You are taller than I*. *Than* is a **conjunction** and *I* is the **subject** of the (reduced) **clause**: *I am*.
- *None of us want to go* is incorrect. *None* is a singular **pronoun**, so *None of us wants to go*.
- Do not say: *I didn't say nothing*. Say: *I didn't say anything*. You can't use a double negative because two negatives make a positive.

Notice that these 'rules-as-regulations' make certain questionable claims. Why, for example, is *than* a **conjunction** and not a **preposition**? Who says that *none* is singular? Or they appeal to logic, as if language was modelled on mathematics. Notice, too, that the application of such rules often produces sentences that sound contrived and unusual.

A descriptive grammar, on the other hand, aims to describe language as it is actually used. To this end, descriptive grammarians draw on corpora (the plural of *corpus*), i.e. digitally-stored databases of attested language use. However, even descriptive grammarians have to make decisions as to what language is standard versus non-standard. While most teaching grammars would prefer *You are taller than me*, few would accept *I didn't say nothing*.

Also, learners are aware that language projects certain values: knowing 'good style' is part of learning the target language culture. So, there may be a place for judicious doses of the prescriptive medicine.

Are British and American grammars really different?

'You say *tomayto* and I say *tomahto*.' The two major varieties of English differ, of course, in their pronunciation. And in many of their word choices. But their grammar?

First of all, it needs to be emphasized that there are not two monolithic varieties of English, one on each side of the Atlantic Ocean. What is loosely classed as British English (BrE) includes a wide range of regional and social varieties, each distinguished by their own phonological, lexical and grammatical features. Similar variety characterizes American English (AmE). Speakers of both subscribe to the idea of there being a standard (even if they themselves don't speak it), i.e. a widely distributed variety associated with education and broadcasting, and which serves as the model for teaching to English language learners.

So, how are these two standard varieties different, grammatically speaking? The main differences that might have implications for the teaching of English are the following:

- the AmE preference for the past simple over the present perfect with *just, already,* and *yet,* as in *Did you have brunch yet?* (AmE);
- the form of some past tense **verbs**, where AmE uses *-ed* for the past of *learn, spell, burn, dream,* etc. (cf. BrE *learnt, spelt, burnt, dreamt*), and where AmE has retained some irregular past **tense** forms such as *dove* (BrE *dived*) and *pled* (*pleaded*);
- *get* has two past **participles** in AmE, *got* and *gotten*, each with a different meaning: *I've got that book at home* [= I have it] v *I've just gotten a new book* [= I have acquired it];
- AmE prefers to use collective **nouns** (*the government, the team*) in the singular, whereas BrE allows *the government are…*;
- the disappearance, in AmE, of the forms *shall/shan't* and their replacement with *will/won't*.

Prescriptive grammarians (see **2**) are also more insistent, in the US, on using the so-called subjunctive in certain constructions (see **69**), and on not using *which* in restrictive clauses: *The rule which I just broke is ridiculous!*

5 Is there a difference between spoken and written grammar?

It used to be thought that the grammar of spoken language mirrored the grammar of written language. But does it?

Speaking, unlike most writing, happens spontaneously. This means planning and production are happening at the same time, and this constrains the degree of grammatical complexity that is feasible. Moreover, most speaking is interactive, and this is reflected in its construction. Here, for example, is an extract of naturally-occurring talk from the Cambridge English Corpus:

1 I was talking to somebody who was a vegetarian and they know I'm on this diet and that I've lost this weight and stuff and they said for them to go back to grease was what did them in.
2 Uh-huh. Well and our son can't eat grease period.
3 Oh.
4 He and grease just ...
5 Really?
6 He can't eat grease. Yeah.
7 We don't fry meat. I do ... I like my egg fried in butter and that's what we had tonight. I had eggs and ham and anyway I fried it in butter and I like that really well and uh that doesn't seem to bother me so I don't know what ...

Features of the spontaneity include a tendency to produce short sequences linked by the **conjunctions** *and, so, but* (Turns 1 and 7); to attach 'tails' to utterances (*period, Yeah*); the use of formulaic language (*so I don't know what*) and vague language (*and stuff*); incomplete utterances and false starts (Turns 4 and 7), and filled pauses (*uh*).

Arguably, these features are not common in written language; nor are some characteristics of written language much used in spoken language, which raises the question as to whether teaching only written grammar is the best preparation for speaking.

Is grammar learned in a set order?

> The assumption underlying most teaching syllabuses is that the order in which grammar items are taught is the order in which they are learned. But is this really true?

Traditionally, and to this day, the items in a grammar syllabus are typically sequenced in terms of *utility* and *difficulty*. The utility of an item is a measure of its likely usefulness for the learner: highly frequent structures like the present simple are clearly more useful than relatively rare structures like the third conditional.

An item's difficulty is calculated on the basis of its structural complexity – simple structures like the present simple are taught before more complex ones, like the present perfect continuous. Difficulty can also be conceptual: a concept like countability (as in *one dog, two dogs*) is considered easier than a concept like definiteness (*a dog* v *the dog*). Finally, an item might be more or less difficult according to whether it has a counterpart in the learner's first language (L1). A learner whose L1 doesn't have **auxiliary verbs** will find these difficult.

Underlying these principles is the assumption that the order in which items are taught will be reflected in the order in which they are learned.

However, research has since shown that learners seem to follow their own 'built-in syllabus' independently of their L1, and irrespective of the teaching order. So, all learners seem to master plural forms before the possessive *'s* (*the dog's breakfast*), and irregular **verbs** (*went, saw*) before regular ones (*worked, looked*). These findings challenge the view that teaching can directly influence learning.

More recently still, research has shown that the built-in syllabus varies according to the learner's L1. So learners who have no **articles** in their L1 (as in Russian) will acquire articles (*a, the*) later and in a different order than learners whose L1 has this feature.

So yes, there is a set order for grammar acquisition, but it is strongly influenced by the learner's L1.

How is grammar best taught?

> The role of grammar in the curriculum is hotly debated.
> How it should be taught is equally contentious.

A grammar describes the rules of the language. It follows (so it was thought) that the best way to teach it is to explain these rules and then practise them. Such practice might typically involve translating sentences in and out of the target language. This is the kind of scholastic approach that dominated the teaching of classical languages, like Latin and Greek, and, to a certain extent persists in the teaching of modern languages. Many self-study courses and digital apps subscribe closely to this system.

A radically different approach attempts to simulate the natural way we learn our first language, by immersion in the processes of using language and thereby getting a feel for it. This more experiential approach rejects the explicit teaching of rules and the use of translation.

The characteristics of these two extremes can be summed up like this:

the scholastic approach	the natural approach
academic	experiential
explicit instruction	implicit learning
bilingual	monolingual
rule learning (deductive)	rule discovery (inductive)
focus on written language	focus on spoken language
focus on accuracy	focus on fluency

The history of language teaching has swung between these two extremes. Nowadays, there is a greater tolerance for features of both. So, for example, experiences of language in use might be combined with explicit instruction; giving rules might be combined with discovering them. The exact blend will depend on such factors as the learners' characteristics and the grammar item itself – some more complex items are more easily taught, while others are better simply picked up.

What is the point of rules?   **8**

> Rules are a useful aid to learning – but only if they are reliable. So many grammar rules seem unreliable because they have exceptions.

Grammar rules are not like road rules: they are not *regulations,* but more like *regularities.* That is, they describe the patterns and combinations that occur in real language use. Some rules are purely about form: *Use the indefinite **article** an before words that begin with a vowel sound*: an ice cream. Other rules relate specific forms to specific meanings: *We use the present simple with **verbs** like* have, love, want, *to talk about states*: I love ice cream.

But language is a living thing: these patterns change. For example, a pattern for asking questions that was common in Shakespeare's day is to invert the **verb** and the **subject**:

> Parolles: Why think you so? (*All's Well That Ends Well*)

At the same time, a new pattern using **auxiliary verbs** was emerging:

> Rosalind: Do you think so? (*As you Like it*)

Eventually, the new pattern prevailed. Exceptions to rules are often evidence that a change is taking place. Or that the rule has not yet been generalized to all cases, as in the case of irregular verbs.

Sometimes, the exceptions are not really exceptions at all, but evidence of a more general rule. For example, the rule about **state verbs** (above) cannot easily accommodate an example like *I'm loving it!* unless we change the rule so that it is more elastic. (See **55** for an explanation.)

The fact that rules are not 100% reliable does not mean they are useless, so long as we recognize that they are less regulations than 'rules of thumb'.

9 Is there grammar 'beyond the sentence'?

Grammar is concerned with the way that words combine to form sentences. But is grammar only about sentences?

Until recently, grammar was concerned exclusively with sentences, especially of the written and invented variety. With the advent of **discourse** analysis, however, the angle widened to embrace whole texts and the way they achieve internal **cohesion**. Their sentences are connected and sequenced in ways that are regular and predictable.

Take, for example, this short text in a London tube station:

> *Going to Covent Garden?*
>
> Covent Gdn Station gets very busy at weekends and in the evenings. But you can avoid the crowds by walking there from Holborn or Leicester Square. The short walk is clearly signposted above ground and maps are on display at both stations.

(Copyright © Transport for London.)

The text, like many public notices, has a problem-solution structure. The negative implication of the phrase *very busy* is contrasted (using the linker *But*) with the positive *can avoid the crowds*. The fact that the walk is *short* and *clearly signposted* also has positive connotations. This, and the way the reader is directly addressed as *you*, helps us infer the writer's intention, i.e. advice. The writer seems to be saying, 'this is *our* solution to *your* problem.' Note also that the last sentence is not easily understood on its own, since it uses specific **determiners** to reference the sentence before it: <u>the</u> *short walk*; <u>both</u> *stations*.

In short, the text displays structural and grammatical features that extend beyond the individual sentences, supporting the argument that grammar should be taught and practised in its contexts of use.

Is there a core grammar?

It's generally accepted that some words are more useful than others, and that for teaching purposes, a core vocabulary is a worthwhile goal. But is there such a thing as a core grammar as well?

Core words are chosen on the basis of – among other things – their frequency, the range of contexts in which they are used, and whether or not there are workable alternatives. Can choices about grammar be based on similar criteria?

Certainly, we now have much more detailed information on frequency and range, thanks to **corpus** linguistics. We know, for example, that **verbs** in the present **tense** are more frequent than either past tense or **modal verbs,** especially in spoken language, and that simple verb forms (*I eat*) are more common than verb forms marked for **aspect** (*I am eating; I have eaten*). We also know that **passive** forms are relatively uncommon, apart from in academic texts, and that, of the modal verbs, *will* is the most frequent, and *shall* the least.

This kind of information is useful, if not for defining a core grammar, at least for setting some short- and mid-term goals. After all, even native speakers do not use all the resources of their first language. And now that English is well established as a language of international communication, some re-positioning of the goalposts may be in order. Do L2 English users really need the luxury of two ways of talking about the past, as in *I went to Sweden once* and *I've been to Sweden once*?

Furthermore, there is a case for arguing that a core vocabulary – especially of high frequency function words – correlates closely with a core grammar. As Dave Willis puts it: 'The commonest patterns in English occur again and again with the commonest words in English'. Maybe we should teach the 'little words' and let the grammar take care of itself.

Willis, D. (1990) *The Lexical Syllabus: a new approach to language teaching*. London: Collins ELT.

B: Nouns, pronouns, articles, adjectives

Nouns are the most common word class in most languages, including English, where they outnumber verbs two to one, or even more in some registers, such as academic writing. They are typically accompanied by articles and adjectives, and are often replaced by pronouns, so it makes sense to bundle these questions together.

11 What's a noun phrase?
12 Why is *money* uncountable?
13 *My family is* or *my family are*?
14 What are articles?
15 What is the *zero article*?
16 Is there a rule for *the*?
17 *We're getting a dog*: any dog or a specific dog?
18 What is the rule for *some* and *any*?
19 *Few* and *a few*; *fewer* and *less* – when do we use them?
20 Why is it *on the bed*, but *in bed*?
21 When do we use *one* and not *a/an*?
22 What do pronouns do?
23 What part of speech is *my* and *mine*?
24 Is there a gender-neutral pronoun in English?
25 When do we use reflexive pronouns?
26 *This/That/It is not true*. Which?
27 Is it *more common* or *commoner*?
28 Why is it *very angry* but not *very furious*?
29 In *train station*, is *train* an adjective?
30 *The chair leg*, *the chair's leg*, or *the leg of the chair*?
31 In *fried eggs*, is *fried* a verb or an adjective?
32 Is there a rule for the order of adjectives?
33 Is it OK to turn nouns into verbs?

What's a noun phrase? **11**

Or, when is a noun just a noun and when is it a phrase?

Apart from on shopping lists (*coffee, eggs, soap*) or in some book or film titles (*Atonement, Jaws*), it's unusual to find words on their own. Generally we use words in groups – even on shopping lists: *decaf coffee; six eggs; liquid soap…* .

A group of words that forms around a **noun** (or **pronoun**) is called a **noun phrase** (NP). NPs typically function as the **subject** or **object** of the sentence: *Duck soup is good for you. I like duck soup.* The nucleus of the **phrase** is the **head** noun (or pronoun). If the NP is the subject of the sentence, the verb must agree with its head: *One of the eggs is broken. The other five are OK.*

Some NPs consist of a single noun (*We need coffee*), but most are modified in some way for greater precision: *We need some decaf coffee.* Different elements come before and after the head. For example:

	Determiner	Premodification	Head	Postmodification
1		*Hard*	*Times*	
2		*Duck*	*Soup*	
3	*My*	*Best Friend's*	*Wedding*	
4	*The*		*Life*	*of Brian*
5	*A*		*Night*	*at the Opera*
6	*The*		*Spy*	*who Loved Me*

NPs are typically premodified by **adjectives** (1), other nouns – called **noun modifiers** (2), and **genitive** constructions (3). They are typically postmodified by *of* constructions (4); **prepositional phrases** (5) or **relative clauses** (6).

In teaching syllabuses, NPs don't always get as much attention as they deserve, given their importance in the sentence. Also, their formation in English differs significantly from some other languages: not all languages allow noun modifiers. In French, for example, 'duck soup' translates as *soupe de canard*.

12   **Why is _money_ uncountable?**

> Surely you can count money? And why can't we say *She has a long hair?*

Most dictionaries identify **nouns** as being either **countable** or **uncountable**. So *dog, car,* and *emotion* are countable – because they can be pluralized: *one dog, two dogs,* etc. *Water, air,* and *information,* on the other hand, normally cannot.

It's usually obvious if a noun is countable or not. Countable nouns refer to unit-like things that can be clearly separated. Uncountable nouns refer to masses and liquids with no clear boundaries, or to more abstract notions such as *health, knowledge* and *happiness.*

But there are a number of inconsistencies that can cause problems for learners – *money* being one of them. Although we can count money in real life, the noun itself has no plural: what we are counting is dollars or euros. So: *How much money do you have?* but *How many dollars?*

There are a number of other uncountable nouns that learners frequently pluralize: *information, advice, furniture* and *luggage.* For most uncountable nouns there is an equivalent structure that expresses a unit of the 'stuff': *a piece of advice, a loaf of bread, an item of luggage.*

The situation is complicated by the fact that many nouns can be both countable and uncountable, depending on our view of them – as mass or unit: *some coffee, a coffee.* Others include *glass, paper, hair* and so on, as well as many abstract nouns: *emotion, life,* and *experience.*

Whether or not a noun is countable (or is being used countably) impacts on the kinds of **determiner** that can precede it:

	the	*a/an*	*(a) few/little*	*(how) much/many*
singular countable	*the dog*	*a dog*	-	-
plural countable	*the dogs*	-	*(a) few dogs*	*(how) many dogs*
uncountable	*the advice*	-	*(a) little advice*	*(how) much advice*

My family is or *my family are?* 13

> Related to the issue of countability is the grammar of collective nouns, like *family, team, government*. Not to mention other odd things about plurals.

Nouns like *family, team, government* and *class* are known as collective nouns, since they refer to collections of people. We can think of them in two ways: as one group acting in unison, or as a collection of individuals with their own needs, wishes or beliefs. Depending on which view we take, we use singular or plural forms of the **verb** and related **pronouns**, e.g. *they, it*. Likewise, we use *which* or *who* as relative pronouns respectively. (In American English the singular options are preferred.) Here are some examples from the Cambridge English Corpus:

> *This is where I hang out, where my <u>family is</u>.*
> *I am Swedish, but my <u>family are</u> a mixture.*
>
> *The <u>government has</u> agreed to consider the request.*
> *This poll shows that the <u>Government are</u> miles out of step with voters.*
>
> *Our <u>class is</u> filled with really intelligent guys.*
> *The <u>class are</u> soon split into groups of four.*
>
> *The <u>team which does</u> it the quickest gets a point.*
> *The <u>team know they</u> have areas to tighten up on.*

Sometimes a singular verb form can combine with a plural pronoun:

> *The <u>team knows they</u> have good players on the bench.*

A related issue concerns singular nouns used as **quantifiers**, such as *group, number* and *couple*, which are usually considered as plural:

> *A <u>group of boys are</u> sitting in the back singing.*
> *A <u>number of species remain</u> to be identified.*
> *A <u>couple of friends have</u> seen it and say it's a hoot!*

What are articles?

> Articles comprise the smallest and most frequent words in the language – but what do they do?

Compare these two sentences, one without an **article** (or **zero article**: see 15) and one with the indefinite article *a*:

> *I had chicken for lunch.* v *I had a chicken for lunch.*

Clearly the article allows us to distinguish between 'chicken-the-stuff' and 'chicken-the-whole-thing'. Compare with:

> *There was glass on the floor.* v *There was a glass on the floor.*

In the case of the following, however, no such distinction can be inferred: *I had the chicken for lunch.* Here, the speaker is identifying the chicken (whether stuff or thing) as being known to the hearer: 'You know which chicken I mean'. The definite article *the* flags the chicken as being 'given information', i.e. a part of the speaker and hearer's shared knowledge. *I had a chicken* makes no such assumption. Compare:

> *Have you fed the cat?* (= You know which cat I mean: presumably the one who shares our space.)

> *She is the bride of Frankenstein.* (= You know which bride I mean: the one of Frankenstein.)

Finally, look at this: *Which came first: the chicken or the egg?*

Here the chicken is not a specific chicken but the representative of its class. We could equally say: *Which came first: chickens or eggs?*

So articles allow us to distinguish between masses and units, between new and shared information and to make general statements about classes of things. How could we manage without them?

What is the *zero article*?

> We are told that there are three articles in English: the indefinite article *a/an*, the definite article *the*, and the zero article. But how can nothing mean something?

The following (invented) text is notable for having no **articles**. Or, rather, for having several instances of the **zero article** (often written Ø), defined as the absence of an article (or any other **determiner**) before a **noun**:

> On Ø Tuesday Ø Robin went to Ø school by Ø bus, did Ø history and Ø French, had Ø fish and Ø chips for Ø lunch, came home, watched Ø TV, drank Ø milk, and went to Ø bed. Ø Life can be dull!

(Note that here *home* doesn't even take a **preposition**, so it's not really a noun at all but an **adverb**.)

When do we use the Ø?

- With **uncountable** concrete **noun**s (see **12**), that are not identified or quantified, i.e. are indefinite: Ø *fish*, Ø *milk*
- With indefinite plural **countable nouns**: Ø *chips*
- With uncountable abstract nouns that are not defined or modified: Ø *history*, Ø *French*, Ø *Life*
- With proper names: Ø *Robin*
- With days, months and seasons that are not identified: Ø *Tuesday*
- With nouns that denote institutions (but not an identified one), modes of transport, and customs or routines: Ø *school*, Ø *bus*, Ø *lunch*, Ø *TV*, Ø *bed* (see also **20**).

Note how the same nouns can take articles when they are specified or identified in some way:

> On <u>the</u> Tuesday before her exam, <u>the</u> Robin who lives upstairs (not <u>the</u> Robin who is my cousin) took <u>a</u> city bus to <u>the</u> local school, studied <u>the</u> history of Mexico, and had <u>a</u> lunch of fish and chips. <u>The</u> fish was off.

16   Is there a rule for *the*?

> Look at any student grammar and you'll find a long list of rules for the definite article, along with an equally long list of exceptions. But is there no general rule that covers all instances?

Communication is more effective if speakers can coordinate the current state of their knowledge. One way they do this is by pointing to the thing they are referring to: *Let's take that bus* is more direct than *There's a bus coming down the street: let's take it.*

Another way they do this is by using the definite **article** *the*. When you use *the,* you are pointing with language. You may be pointing at something in the real world: *Here comes the bus!* More often you are pointing at something in your shared knowledge. *Let's take the bus* is another way of saying *You know that bus we both have in common: let's take it.*

How do we know what *the* is pointing to? In other words, how does knowledge become shared? We can share things in the immediate context (*Pass the milk*) or in our shared world (*Have you seen the keys?*) or in the wider world that we inhabit (*The buses are on strike*). In every case, when I use *the,* I'm assuming you know what I'm pointing to.

The same applies, of course, to things that are unique: *The moon is full.* You don't even have to look to know which moon.

Often, the referent to which *the* is pointing has been mentioned earlier, or can be inferred from a prior mention: *A dog approached. The beast was growling.* Or from the context: *We took a taxi. The driver didn't speak English.*

Or the referent is specified by **modifiers** of the **noun**, either before or after it: *the Queen of Sheba; the oldest woman in the world.*

Most occurrences of *the* can be explained by reference to shared knowledge. The main 'exceptions' relate mainly to proper nouns and are probably best learned as individual items.

We're getting a dog: any dog or a specific dog?

> Some grammars claim you use the indefinite article when you refer to a single, non-specific thing: *I saw a lion at the zoo.* But, surely, it was a specific lion?

Look at this example:

1 *We're going to get Lucy a dog for her birthday.*

The dog is indefinite – signaled by the use of the indefinite **article** *a* (see **14**), because this is its first mention: it is not a dog that has been mentioned before or is otherwise familiar to the person being addressed. But is the speaker thinking of a specific dog, or simply one as yet unspecified member of the class *DOG*? The answer is that – without more context – we don't know. Let's add more context:

1a *We're going to get Lucy <u>a dog</u>. We chose <u>it</u> yesterday.*
1b *We're going to get Lucy <u>a dog</u>. We're going to place an advert for <u>one</u>.*

In the case of 1a, the dog is a specific dog – it has already been chosen and the speaker has a very clear mental image of it. In the case of 1b, it is any one of the class of things called *DOG*: it is both indefinite and non-specific. The clue is in the **pronouns** in the sentences that follow: *it* v *one*. *It* is specific; *one* is simply one of a class.

Here are some more examples:

> *Is there <u>a doctor</u> on the plane? We need <u>one</u>.* (= non-specific)
> *I sat next to <u>a doctor</u> on the plane. I think you know <u>her</u>.* (= specific)

The ambiguous nature of the indefinite article, i.e. that it can be used with both specific and non-specific reference, accounts for the humour in this joke:

> In the US a person gets hit by a car every 5 minutes. And he's getting mighty sick of it!

18 What is the rule for *some* and *any*?

> Is there a difference between *Do you want some milk?* and *Do you want any milk?* If so, what's the rule?

The accepted view is that when you are talking about **uncountable nouns** (see **12**), or plural **countable nouns** you use *some* for affirmative statements, and *any* for negative ones and for questions:

1 *We need some sugar/eggs.*
2 *We don't have any sugar/eggs.*
3 *Do we have any sugar/eggs?*

This rule works in most cases, but it needs to be refined a little to take into account the difference between sentences (4) and (5) and between sentences (6) and (7) below:

4 *I don't like some shellfish.*
5 *I don't like any shellfish.*
6 *Do you need some money?*
7 *Do you need any money?*

In all these cases, *some* and *any* act as quantifying **determiners**: they answer the question *How much?* In the case of *some*, the quantity is vague but limited: in (4) there are a number of shellfish I don't like, but there are others that I do. Likewise, in (6) I am thinking about a limited, although imprecise, amount of money.

Any, on the other hand, is unlimited: it means all or none. In (5) there are no shellfish that I like, and in (7) I am not limiting the amount of money you may need. (The same distinction applies to the difference between *anyone* and *someone*, by the way.)

Few and *a few*; *fewer* and *less* – when do we use them?

> Grammar purists criticize signs in supermarkets saying '10 items or less'. But is that fair?

(*A*) *few* and *fewer* and (*a*) *little* and *less* are all quantifying **determiners**: that is, they go before **nouns** and express small quantities.

So this is what the pedagogical grammars might say:

- Use (*a*) *few* and *fewer* with **countable nouns**: *a few years; fewer clients*
- Use (*a*) *little, less/least* with **uncountable nouns**: *a little work; little hope; less traffic; least interest*

A few and *a little* have positive meanings, like *some*, whereas *few* and *little* have the negative meaning of 'less than expected' or 'not many':

> There were <u>a few students</u> in the audience. ~ Oh, <u>that's nice</u>.
> There were <u>few students</u> in the audience. ~ Oh, <u>that's a shame</u>.

So *ten items or less* or *ten items or fewer*? Current usage suggests that the *fewer/less* distinction is collapsing, even in some formal registers. Here are some examples from the Cambridge English Corpus:

> A single project will displace <u>less people</u>.
> Bilinguals produced <u>less errors</u> than the native Spanish speakers.
> The cathedral had <u>no less than ten portals</u>.

This development may partly owe to the fact that numeral + noun combinations describing time periods or distances take *less* rather than *fewer*:

> The building was <u>less than ten years old</u>. (not *fewer*)
> He had moved <u>less than five kilometres</u>. (not *fewer*)

20 Why is it *on the bed*, but *in bed*?

> Or, more generally, is there a reason why certain nouns like *work, foot, train, school* and so on don't take an article?

Why does a child's alphabet say *A is for Apple*, and not *A is for an Apple* or *A is for the Apple* or *A is for Apples*? Put another way, what happens when we strip a **noun** of all its **determiners**, **modifiers** and plural suffixes? What we have left is the bare concept – the essence, if you like: not *an apple, a green apple, the apples*, but just *apple*. Of course, we can use this bare noun to represent the uncountable stuff – *apple,* as in the stuff in an apple pie. But it goes further than this. *A is for Apple* stands for 'apple-ness', the idea of apple.

This is most obvious with abstract **uncountable nouns** (see **12**), as in *Beauty is truth, truth beauty …* (Keats, *Ode on a Grecian Urn*).

But it also works for **countable nouns**, when we are thinking of them as almost an abstract idea. Thus, the cat can be *on the bed* – on a specific bed. But when we say that a person is *in bed*, we are not envisaging a specific bed so much as the idea of rest, of sleep, of not being *out of bed*. The same goes for a number of other daily routines and common institutions that have been abstracted from the physical world and turned into ideas: *at work, to school, in hospital, in prison, by bus, on foot, at sea,* and so on.

Of course, when we are thinking of the place itself, we can use an **article** (see **14**) and specify it in some way. There is a difference between:

> *He went to hospital to have his appendix out.*

and

> *He went to the hospital to deliver the linen.*

This abstracting function of the **zero article** (see **15**) also appears on signs, e.g. *SCHOOL*, or *HOSPITAL*, where it is irrelevant which school or hospital is being referred to.

When do we use *one* and not *a/an*? 21

> Both *a/an* and *one* are determiners (they precede and limit the reference of nouns) and both are used with singular countable nouns. So, what's the difference?

Learners frequently confuse *a/an* and *one*, as in these examples of incorrect usage from the Cambridge English Corpus:

1   *I'm working for <u>one regional bank</u>.*
2   *Every human being has <u>one different story</u> to tell.*
3   *After about <u>one quarter of an hour</u> you will be in the centre.*
4   *I usually stay in Germany for <u>a month per year</u>.*
5   *There was <u>only a problem</u>, it cost too much.*
6   *You will need <u>only a ticket</u> per person.*

Examples 1 – 3 demonstrate overuse of *one*, while 4 – 6 show the reverse. So, what's the rule?

The default **determiner** is *a/an*: *one* is used mainly when emphasis needs to be given to the number, e.g. to contrast one with another, or to mean not two or more:

> *There was <u>only one problem</u> …*

One is also used to draw attention to a unique feature of a narrative or description, as in these examples from the **corpus**:

> *And when he was about 12 there was <u>one teacher</u> that suddenly realized that my son was very, very capable.*
> *If you're in New Orleans, there's <u>one place</u> you're sure to find it.*
> *There was <u>one time</u> – it was a Saturday – and we went shopping.*

One (plural *ones*) is also a **pronoun** and is used to replace a previous **countable noun**:

> *You have a <u>bathing suit</u>? ~ Last year I bought <u>one</u>. ~ I have to get <u>one</u>.*

> Pronouns, we are told, can replace nouns. But is it always the case that there is a noun that the pronoun stands for?

There are at least six different kinds of **pronouns** in this email:

> *I*'ve attached a couple more photos of *what I* noticed on Sunday so *you* can see for *yourself*, but *they*'re not very clear - *it*'s a bit difficult to see clean water against a white wall! *We* were not alone in experiencing *this*. Pablo knocked on *our* door and told *us* that other flats both above and below *ours* had been more seriously flooded. *I* don't know if *anyone* has contacted the administrators yet.

They are:

- personal and possessive pronouns: *I, you; my, yours*
- reflexive pronoun: *yourself*
- relative pronoun: *what*
- demonstrative pronoun: *this*
- indefinite pronoun: *anyone*

Very few of these pronouns can be easily replaced by a **noun**. The personal pronouns (*I, you, our*) and reflexive pronouns (*yourself*), for example, stand for people known to the writer and reader. The pronoun *it* (as in <u>*it*</u>*'s a bit difficult*) stands for a whole **clause** (*to see clean water*, etc.).

Likewise, demonstrative pronouns (*this/that*) can refer to previously mentioned content (*… in experiencing <u>this</u>*), or to the immediate context (*Look at <u>that</u>!*). Relative pronouns link a **relative clause** to the preceding **noun phrase** (*the spy <u>who</u> loved me*), or introduce a noun clause (*<u>what</u> I noticed*). And indefinite pronouns (*anyone, something*) are, by definition, vague, and so not easily replaced by a noun phrase.

In the above text, the only pronouns that can be easily identified as standing for a noun phrase are *they* (= *the photos*) and *ours* (= *our flat*).

Perhaps it's better to think of pronouns as having a cohesive function: connecting elements in a text, and connecting a text to its context.

Traditionally, *my* and *mine* are described as possessive pronouns. But which one do we use when?

Learners typically have problems choosing the right form when talking about possession, as in these learner examples:

- *This will save <u>hers</u> and <u>mine time</u>.* (= her time and mine)
- *I also want to see <u>a friend of my</u> who is here.* (= a friend of mine)
- *Every single individual has his/<u>hers</u> rights.* (= his/her)
- *The week before, he had gone with <u>her mother</u> to a cloth shop.* (= with his mother)
- *I was watching a football match with Kevin, <u>a my Italian friend</u>.* (= an Italian friend of mine)

The challenge for the learner is choosing between **determiners** on the one hand and **pronouns** on the other.

	1ˢᵗ person singular	2ⁿᵈ person singular and plural	3ʳᵈ person singular	1ˢᵗ person plural	3ʳᵈ person plural
determiner	*my*	*your*	*his/her/its*	*our*	*their*
pronoun	*mine*	*yours*	*his/hers*	*ours*	*theirs*

Determiners precede the **noun** and are part of the **noun phrase**. The possessive determiners fall into this group. They must always precede a noun: *Is this <u>your</u> towel?* They cannot combine with other determiners: **a my Italian friend*.

Pronouns, on the other hand, can stand on their own, as an independent noun phrase: *Whose is this towel? ~ It's <u>hers</u>.*

A secondary problem is ensuring that the gender and number of the determiner match that of the possessor, not the possessed: *He had gone with his mother.* (Not **her mother.*)

24 Is there a gender-neutral pronoun in English?

> English is lucky in not having articles that are marked as either masculine or feminine. But gender distinctions persist in the pronouns: *he* v *she*; *him* v *her*. Is there any way round this?

This is from a teachers' book written a good while ago: 'A teacher's initial task, normally, is to organise his material. This means that he has first to determine what he is to teach … '. And, later in the same book, 'Once the pupil has been trained to read, he is virtually independent of the teacher' (Morris, 1964). An exclusively male world?

Well, at the time it was argued that *he* and *his* were gender-neutral **pronouns**, and applied equally to males and females. This argument no longer holds water. A reaction to the inherent sexism of *he/his* has been to use *she* and *her*, especially when speaking about teachers, the majority of whom, after all, are female. So Peter Medgyes (1994/2017) writes: 'It is very difficult for the teacher to look confident when her authority is continually challenged …', and uses the (slightly inelegant) *he/she* and *his/her*: 'The native speaker of English speaks English as his/her first language'.

Attempts have been made to introduce wholly new, gender-neutral pronouns into English, but the last pronoun to establish a foothold in English was *its* in the late 16th century. With closed classes of words (like **prepositions**, pronouns and **articles**) change happens slowly.

Meanwhile, the plural forms *they, their* and *them* – often with singular reference – have been enlisted to fill the gap:

> It's frustrating for the person who can't speak if they're not allowed to.
> If anyone asked me if I liked their haircut, I would reply truthfully.
> The casual observer might easily think themself back in 1945.

Medgyes, P. (1994/2017) *The Non-Native Teacher*. Bridgend: Swan Communication Ltd.

Morris, I. (1964) *The Art of Teaching English as a Living Language*. London: Macmillan.

When do we use reflexive pronouns?

> Reflexive pronouns are obligatory in some contexts, but optional in others. Which are which?

The reflexive **pronouns** are:

Singular: *myself, yourself, himself, herself, itself*
Plural: *ourselves, yourselves, themselves*

There is also the more formal *oneself*: *One must not deceive oneself.*
Themself is used as gender-neutral 3rd person singular (see **24**).

Reflexive pronouns are obligatory with **transitive verbs** when the **subject** and **object** (either direct or indirect) are the same: *Did you hurt yourself?* Typical verbs that take a reflexive pronoun as object are: *injure, take care of, behave, control, excel, prove, excuse, explain, amuse, enjoy, help* and *repeat.*

Reflexives are not necessary with verbs such as *wash, shave,* and *dress,* (*You haven't shaved*) but may be used if the agency of the subject needs to be emphasised: *He cannot shave himself because of hand tremors.*

If a verb or **adjective** is followed by a **preposition** and the object of the preposition is the subject of the **clause**, a reflexive is necessary:

The woman next door is very friendly and I often talk to her.
v *When I am alone at home I often talk to myself.*

Similarly, reflexives are also used after certain **nouns** that have the sense of representation, followed by *of*: *picture, version, image, sense, fool,* and *photo* being the most common:

Most had never seen pictures of themselves.
He felt he had made a fool of himself.

Finally, reflexives are used, optionally, to emphasise the singularity of a person or thing: *I made it myself* means *I alone made it.*

26 *This/That/It is not true. Which?*

> *This here is mine. That there is yours. ~So it is.* In speech, it's often clear what we are referring to and which pronoun to use. But not always.

This and *that*, and their plural forms *these* and *those*, are **demonstratives** – they 'point' using language: *What's that? Whose is this phone?* They can stand on their own, as **pronouns**, or precede **nouns**, as **determiners**. Essentially, they contrast near and distant reference points. *How much are these?* (= near me). *Give me some of those.* (= over there). They contrast with *it/they*, which are neutral with regard to distance: *How much are they?*

However, they are also commonly used in both speech and writing to point, not at things, but at previously mentioned ideas and propositions. But the idea of nearness and distance is retained, as in these examples:

1 *We don't have mountains in Texas though.*
  ~ Well, <u>this</u> is true. (= speaker is 'close' to the proposition)
2 *So he took your money, Frank, and didn't do the job.*
  ~No, I'm telling you, <u>that</u>'s not true. (= distance)

That is very frequent in speech. However, as a referring device, *this* is more common than *that* in academic writing:

3 *Not all application fields are equally represented. We expect that <u>this</u> is due to two factors …*
4 *Consonant sequences h-nasal are prohibited in Tariana; <u>this</u> explains the change from -hma to -mha.*

Note that in (3) and (4) *it* would not work as well as *that*. *It* is used to reiterate an already mentioned topic:

5 *<u>The effect of the biting</u> by e. g. a snake or a scorpion is not due to the incision of the spur or the fang: rather, <u>it</u> is due to the venom.*

Is it *more common* or *commoner*?

> The comparison of adjectives takes the form of adding *-er* or by using *more*, according to the length of the word. But what about medium-sized words?

According to the Cambridge English Corpus, *more common* is around 25 times more common than *commoner*. On the other hand, *happier* is over 30 times more common than *more happy*.

1 *Fog is often <u>more common</u> along rivers than in nearby fields.*
2 *Colds are <u>commoner</u> in winter months.*
3 *Extroverts are <u>more happy</u> than introverts.*
4 *I'm <u>happier</u> now than I ever was in my tennis career.*

As a number of grammars note, while both possibilities exist, it depends on the ending: **adjectives** ending in *-y* (*happy, easy, sunny*), *-le* (*little, simple, feeble*), and *-ow* (*narrow, yellow*) favour *-er*: *happier, simpler, narrower,* etc. On the other hand, those ending in a suffix such as *-less, -ful, -ous* (*harmless, useful, jealous*), tend to attract *more*.

Even some one-syllable adjectives form their comparative only with *more*: *You couldn't be more wrong*, not **You couldn't be wronger.* Others are *real* and *right*, and those ending in *-ed* or *-ing*: *more bored.*

But it's not unusual to find other one-syllable adjectives with *more* and it may be because this adds emphasis, or because of the position in the sentence. Here are some more examples:

5 *They are here to make people <u>more safe</u>.*
6 *I have never been <u>more proud</u> to be an American than today.*

On the other hand, gradable one-syllable adjectives, like *short* and *tall, young* and *old, rich* and *poor, wet* and *dry,* almost always take *-er*:

7 *<u>The taller</u> you are, <u>the longer</u> your coat can be.*

28 Why is it *very angry* but not *very furious?*

And what about *quite big* and *quite enormous?*

Adjectives like *good, bad* and *ugly* can be graded. That is to say, they can be arranged along a scale: a movie, for example, can be *quite good, very good* or *extremely good*. These adjectives are known as gradable. Gradable adjectives can have comparative and superlative forms: *good, better, best; ugly, more ugly, most ugly*. They also tend to have opposites, which are also gradable: *good/bad; ugly/beautiful*.

Gradable adjectives can be modified by **adverbs** of degree of the type *very, rather, somewhat, extremely* etc: *we are very angry; she was somewhat annoyed*. But they are not normally modified by adverbs that express totality: **we are utterly angry; *she was absolutely annoyed*.

A smaller number of adjectives describe absolute qualities which cannot normally be arranged on a scale: they are ungradable, e.g. *human, dead, married, female*. Many of these adjectives describe absolute states: *perfect, unique, impossible, awful*. These are modified by adverbs that are also absolute: *absolutely perfect, utterly unique, totally awful*, but not usually **very perfect, *extremely awful*.

Many common gradable adjectives have an ungradable equivalent which can be used for the purposes of emphasis or exaggeration:

> *it's very <u>cold</u>* → *it's absolutely <u>freezing</u>*
> *she was very <u>angry</u>* → *she was totally <u>furious</u>*

Likewise, many ungradable adjectives that describe categories can be made gradable, so as to describe qualities:

> *The use of <u>digital</u> technologies ... The world is becoming <u>more digital</u>*.

Finally, note that the adverb *quite* has two different meanings, depending on whether it is used with gradable or ungradable adjectives:

> gradeable: *the portions were quite big* (= rather or somewhat big)
> ungradeable: *the portions were quite enormous* (= totally enormous)

In *train station*, is *train* an adjective?   29

> And, if it's a noun, why isn't it plural: **a trains station?*
> After all, it serves more than one train.

The **head noun** of a **noun phrase** (see **11**) is typically pre-modified in some way, either to describe the noun or to classify it:

1 *the new station*   2 *Central Station*

In both these cases, the pre-modifier is an **adjective**. Adjectives can typically come before a noun (*the new station*), or they can follow the noun after a linking **verb**, like *be*: *the station is new*. Adjectives can also be qualified by degree **adverbs**: *The station is very central*. And they have comparative and superlative forms: *newer, newest; more/most central*.

But there are other ways of classifying a noun. One very common way is through the use of **noun modifiers** (or noun classifiers) as in:

3 *The train station*   4 *The Finland Station*

In these cases, the modifier tells us what type or class of noun we are talking about: a *train station* as opposed to a *bus station*, for example. *Train* is not an adjective because it doesn't fulfil any of the adjective 'tests' mentioned above:

> *a train station* → **the station is train*
> *a train station* → **a very train station*
> *a train station* → **a trainer station*

Nouns used to classify other nouns are not usually pluralized: *train station,* not **trains station*; *shoe store,* not **shoes store*.

Noun modifiers are an extremely productive feature of English, and account for the high density of nouns that are typical of academic writing in particular, e.g. *The MAGPIE (multipurpose automated genome project investigation environment) genome annotation system was also applied.*

30 *The chair leg, the chair's leg, or the leg of the chair?*

> In Old English, nouns were marked according to gender, class, case, and number. None of this complicated system has survived, except the plural ending -s, and the genitive 's. Even so, the genitive 's still causes problems.

Here are some learner errors from the Cambridge English Corpus:

a   *We went to <u>the house of my brother</u>. (= my brother's house)*
b   *Titti was getting down because of <u>the dog absence</u>. (= the dog's absence)*
c   *In London we could go to a <u>friend of my father</u>. (= of my father's)*
d   *Now, <u>my table's leg</u> has been broken. (= the leg of my table)*
e   *Usually, we have <u>a month holiday</u>. (= a month's holiday)*
f   *I want to become <u>a computer's engineer</u>. (= a computer engineer)*
g   *I went to <u>a shop of clothes</u> yesterday. (= a clothes shop)*

While more than one choice may be possible, here are some simplified rules that explain the corrections:

1   Where the first **noun** is a person and the second noun is a thing possessed by that person, the **genitive** *'s* (also called possessive *'s*) is preferred → examples a: *my brother's house* and b: *the dog's absence*
2   A double genitive is used when the possessor is a person and the thing or person possessed is indefinite (*a/an*). → c: *of my father's*
3   Where the possessor is inanimate, an *of*-**phrase** is preferred. → d: *the leg of my table*
4   With some common time expressions, *'s* is used → e: *a month's holiday*
5   A **noun modifier** (noun + noun) is used where the first noun classifies the second noun. → f: *a computer engineer*, g: *a clothes shop*

So *John's leg* and *the dog's leg*. But *the leg of the chair*, or *the chair leg*.

In *fried eggs*, is *fried* a verb or an adjective?

Many adjectives ending in -*ing* or -*ed* started life as the participles of verbs: *charming, embarrassing, interested, tired*. But what about the borderline cases?

Just to remind you, **verbs** have two **participles**: the -*ing* form, and the -*ed* form. So, the participles of a regular verb like *fry* are *frying* and *fried*; and, of an irregular verb, like *break*: *breaking* and *broken*.

Generally, it is quite clear that the participle is functioning like a verb:

> *I'm <u>frying</u> eggs.*
> *Someone has <u>broken</u> the handle.*
> *The picture is <u>breaking</u> up.*

Other examples are less clear:

> *How do you like your eggs? <u>Boiled</u> or <u>fried</u>?*
> *The handle is <u>broken</u>.*
> *<u>Breaking</u> news.*

One test is if the -*ing* or -*ed* word can be modified by *very*, in which case it is an **adjective** (see **29**): *very interested, very embarrassing*. But not **very fried* or **very breaking*. Conversely, if the participle can be modified by *much* or *well*, or an **adverb** that expresses a process, it is more likely a verb: *a well boiled egg; rapidly breaking news*.

The situation is complicated by the fact that many -*ing* words have become **nouns** – *swimming, painting, cooking* (see **40**) – and frequently modify other nouns: *a <u>swimming</u> pool, a <u>cooking</u> program*. So, there is a difference between *a frying egg* (= an egg which is frying, i.e. *frying* is a verb) and *a frying pan* (= a pan for frying, i.e. *frying* is a noun).

Without context, it is often difficult to decide: *This fish needs <u>frying</u>*. Noun or verb? Try this test:

> *This fish needs more <u>frying</u>.* (It's a noun.)
> *This fish needs <u>frying</u> more.* (It's a verb.)

32 Is there a rule for the order of adjectives?

> 'Stacking' of adjectives – i.e. creating long strings of them –
> is relatively rare. But one or two adjectives in a row is
> quite common. What's the rule?

If you read novels, the following descriptive style may be familiar:

> I had called upon my friend, Mr. Sherlock Holmes, one day in the
> autumn of last year and found him in deep conversation with a very
> stout, florid-faced, elderly gentleman with fiery red hair. ... Our visitor
> bore every mark of being an average commonplace British tradesman
> ... He wore rather baggy grey shepherd's check trousers, a not over-
> clean black frock-coat, and a drab waistcoat with a heavy brassy
> Albert chain ... A frayed top-hat and a faded brown overcoat with a
> wrinkled velvet collar lay upon a chair beside him.
> (Conan Doyle, *The Adventures of Sherlock Holmes.*)

What determines the order in these long adjectival strings? Here are a
few rules of thumb:

1 **adverbs** precede the **adjectives** they modify: *very stout, rather baggy*
2 adjectives precede **noun modifiers,** such as those describing the type
   or material: *a heavy brassy Albert chain; a wrinkled velvet collar*
3 evaluative adjectives precede more factual adjectives: *average
   commonplace British tradesman; a not over-clean black frock-coat*
4 colour adjectives tend to follow other adjectives: *fiery red hair; a
   faded brown overcoat*
5 size adjectives precede age or shape: *a very stout, florid-faced, elderly
   gentleman*

To summarize, Cowan (2008) proposes the following order:

1 article or number; 2 opinion; 3 size; 4 shape; 5 condition; 6 age; 7
colour; 8 origin/material; 9 head noun

Cowan, R. (2008). *The Teacher's Grammar of English.* Cambridge: Cambridge University
Press.

We happily talk about *buttering bread, watering plants, or papering over cracks*, so why should we mind when someone uses *friend* as a verb? Or *impact*? Or *action*?

Turning words of one word class (see **74**) into another, without any change to the form of the word, such as the addition of prefixes or suffixes, is called conversion. For example, the **preposition** *up* becomes a **verb** in the sentence *they upped the price*, and a **noun** in *ups and downs*. Conversion is a highly productive word formation process and one with a long history. In fact, Shakespeare himself uses *friend* as a verb: *I know that we shall have him well to friend*. (*Julius Caesar*)

The conversion of nouns into verbs is one of the most common ways of repurposing(!) words and has given us the verbs *to butter, to water,* and *to paper*, among countless others. Up to a fifth of verbs in English started life as nouns or **adjectives**, according to one estimate (Pinker, 2014). Body parts in particular lend themselves to being 'verbed': *he shouldered the load, she elbowed her way to the front, she heads her own company, who's going to foot the bill?* etc. Certain constructions encourage creative conversions: *I'm all partied out. I'm all pizza'd out,* etc. And technology has provided a host of new verbs: *to text, to message, to google, to skype,* etc.

The direction of conversion need not be one way: verbs can be converted to nouns: *a hug, a swim, a drive, a cheat, a spy,* and so on.

Nevertheless, the coining(!) of new verbs from nouns or other parts of speech can be a source of irritation for many purists, especially when existing words have been supplanted by a new coinage. Why *to friend* when there is a verb *to befriend*?

Despite these complaints, conversion is too productive a word formation process to be easily 'unfriended'.

Pinker, S. (2014). *The Sense of Style*. New York: Allen Lane.

C: Verb forms

For better or worse, verbs occupy a major chunk of the English language curriculum. In the first of three sections devoted to them, this one looks at the way English verbs are formed – their auxiliaries, their infinitives, and so on – and the way that they combine with other elements to form phrasal verbs and conditional constructions, among other things.

If you ever studied Latin you'll probably have learned by heart the conjugation of the verb *amare* (to love): *amo, amas, amat ...*, etc. Why is English *not* like Latin?

A conjugation is the traditional term for a whole class of **verbs** that, in a particular language, are inflected differently. An **inflection** is a word-ending (also known as a kind of *suffix*) that has a specific grammatical function: in English, for example, **nouns** are inflected in the plural by adding -*s*.

French has three verb conjugations: verbs whose **infinitive** ends in -*er*, such as *parler* (to speak); verbs whose infinitive ends in -*ir*, such as *choisir* (to choose); and verbs whose infinitive ends in -*re*, such as *vendre* (to sell). Within each group, the various **tenses** and persons are inflected differently, resulting in scores of different inflections.

Spanish also has three conjugations; modern Greek has two; modern Hebrew has seven.

English has no verb classes analogous to these: there are no conjugations, as such, in English. The nearest English has to conjugations are regular verbs and irregular ones. So we cannot talk about an English verb being conjugated – only inflected. For example, in English the past tense is inflected by adding -*ed* to regular verbs: *walk* → *walked*. To repeat, verbs in English are not conjugated; they are inflected.

It might seem a trivial difference but the notion that English behaves grammatically like Latin, or Latinate languages, such as French and Spanish, has long afflicted English grammatical description, with grammarians tirelessly looking for parallels between English and classical languages. This, in turn, has meant that verbs, and their inflections, are given unmerited emphasis in pedagogical grammars. In fact, the English verb system – compared to French or modern Greek – is relatively uncomplicated (see **2**).

35   **Why are some verbs irregular?**

> How is it that English is burdened with nearly 200 verbs –
> like *speak, read,* and *write* – that are irregular?

In English, regular **verbs** (which are the vast majority) follow the
pattern: *work* (**infinitive**) – *worked* (past **tense**) – *worked* (past
participle). Irregular verbs display a variety of quite different patterns,
e.g. *break – broke – broken,* and *put – put – put.*

The fact that these different patterns coexist owes to the history of
English and its influence by Germanic languages, which distinguished
between strong and weak forms of verbs. In strong verbs, the past tense
was indicated by a change of vowel sound, retained in English *sing →
sang.* The past participle of Germanic verbs ended in *-en,* a feature that
was also retained in many verbs: e.g. *written, given, spoken,* but not in
others, e.g. *run, swum, sung.*

Weak verbs, on the other hand, formed their past forms with *-d* or *-t,*
retained in English regular verbs. For ease of articulation, many of these
were simplified: so, not **hitted,* but *hit,* while others experienced vowel
shortening: not **keeped* but *kept.*

Although many strong forms were regularized over time, the persistence
of irregular verbs owes a lot to their frequency. And some very common
verbs, like the verbs *be* and *go* are highly irregular: *am/is/are – was/were
– been; go – went – gone.*

Nevertheless, there are six general patterns to irregular verbs:

> Class 1: *-ed* changes to *-t: build – built – built.*
> Class 2: *-ed* or *-t* plus vowel change: *mean – meant – meant.*
> Class 3: *-ed* in past, but *–(e)n* in past participle: *show – showed – shown*
> Class 4: vowel change in the past or past participle, or both, plus *-(e)n*
>   in past participle: *give –gave – given; see – saw – seen.*
> Class 5: vowel change in past, past participle or both, no other change:
>   *come – came – come; begin – began – begun.*
> Class 6: no change: *cut – cut – cut.*

Why is the third person -s hard to learn?

Of all the grammatical peculiarities of English, the third person -s (as in *she works*) would seem to be the cruellest.

Here are some errors from the Cambridge Learner Corpus that result from difficulties with the third person -s:

> My boss <u>don't</u> like give me free time, he <u>like</u> give me a lot of work.
> If the dinner <u>start</u> at 7:30, I will be there at 7 pm.
> It's not my. It <u>belong</u> to my sister.
> His father <u>own</u> a very tiny shop which sells computers.
> We go on foot, it's <u>take</u> only 10 minutes.
> So why did the lights <u>goes</u> out?
> I've heard that you <u>works</u> more than 10–12 hours a day.
> My colleagues <u>says</u> I have a unique sense of humour.

The examples show how learners underuse the -s, or – less commonly – overuse it. Research evidence into acquisition orders suggests that it is acquired relatively late – in some cases never. Why?

One reason is that it is hard to hear, especially in some contexts: *She likes skiing.* Another is that it is counter-intuitive: in English and many languages -s is commonly a marker of plurality: *one dog, two dogs.* It doesn't feel right in a singular context. Also, in some European languages, the -s suffix marks the second person singular, not the third: *¿Hablas español?* (Do you speak Spanish?).

Finally, and perhaps most importantly, it is redundant. English, unlike some languages, always requires that **verbs** have **subjects,** and the person and number of the subject is seldom in doubt: <u>His father</u> owns a very tiny shop; <u>It</u> belongs to my sister. The -s adds no more information to what is already there. Indeed, there are some varieties of English, such as in East Anglia in the UK, or in African American vernacular English, that have never seen the need for it.

Indeed, given all of the above, its widespread omission in Lingua Franca English is hardly a cause for alarm.

37 What are auxiliary verbs?

> 'The whole entirely depends ... upon the auxiliary verbs,
> Mr. Yorick. Because with auxiliary verbs you can talk
> about anything. Even a white bear: Have I ever seen one?
> Might I ever have seen one? Am I ever to see one?'
>
> *Tristram Shandy* (Sterne, 1759)

Auxiliary verbs are among the most common words in the language:
they are the so-called 'helping verbs' and combine with main (or lexical)
verbs to express a variety of important meanings. They are:

- the primary auxiliaries: *be, have* and *do*
- the **modal** auxiliaries: *will, would, shall, should, can, could, may, might* and *must*

The primary auxiliaries also function as verbs in their own right: *She is Korean; I have two sisters; Do your homework!* The modal auxiliaries were also once verbs in their own right but, apart from *will* (*She willed him to agree*), they have since lost their independent status.

The primary auxiliaries *be* and *have* combine with **participles** to form verb phrases: *is writing, has written, was written.* (For the functions of *do*, see **41**.) The modal auxiliaries combine with bare **infinitive**: *will write, must write, can write* ... and also with primary auxiliaries to form complex verb phrases: *must have written, can't have been writing* ... . The many auxiliary combinations that are possible make up for the fact that English verbs are largely uninflected (see **2, 34**).

Auxiliary verbs differ from main verbs in that they can be made negative by the addition of *not* (often contracted): *isn't, have not, mustn't, couldn't.* And they invert with their **subject** to form questions: *is it ...? do you ...? might they ...?* Neither of these mechanisms is possible with main verbs: **like not, *like you ...? *works she ...?*

Their syntactic and semantic functions make the auxiliaries among the most important words in the language.

> The so-called *-ing* form describes a wide range of
> phenomena, all of which have the suffix *-ing* in common.
> So what special meaning does *-ing* add to a word?

Words that end in *-ing* cover virtually all word classes. For example, the
-ing form can be used:

- as a **noun**, with a **determiner**: *Have you done the <u>shopping</u>?*
- as an **adjective**: *your <u>loving</u> nephew; It was so <u>embarrassing</u>.*
- as a **conjunction**: *<u>Supposing</u> it rains?*
- as a **preposition**: *I told everyone, <u>including</u> your wife.*
- as the **verb** in a **non-finite (participle)** clause:
  - as the **subject, object**, or **complement** of a verb: *<u>Seeing</u> is <u>believing</u>.
    I don't like <u>waiting</u> in line. Do you remember <u>meeting</u> her?*
  - after verbs of perception plus an object: *She heard a dog <u>barking</u>.*
  - after some adjectives: *That book's not worth <u>reading</u>.*
  - after some prepositions: *This knife is good for <u>slicing</u> tomatoes.
    We talked about <u>fishing</u>. I look forward to <u>meeting</u> you.*
  - as an **adverbial clause**: *He stood <u>breathing</u> heavily.*
  - as a way of modifying a noun: *That person <u>knitting</u> is my neighbour.*
- as a **participle** in a **finite** verb phrase: *Someone was <u>laughing</u>.*

What the *-ing* adds is the idea of there being some activity that is in
progress. This is clearest in cases where there is a non *-ing* alternative:

> *Seeing is believing* v *To see is to believe.*
> *I don't like waiting in line* v *I don't like to wait in line.*
> *She heard a dog barking* v *She heard a dog bark.*
> *Someone was laughing* v *Someone laughed.*

As Broughton (1990) puts it, 'Remember that the *-ing* form, whatever
word class it is operating as, still carries a sense of ongoing activity'.

Broughton, G. (1990) *Penguin English Grammar A – Z for Advanced Students.* London:
Penguin Books.

There are a number of verbs that can take an *-ing* form or
a *to*-infinitive. Is there a difference in meaning? If so, why?

The syntactic patterns that follow certain **verbs** seem quite arbitrary at
times. Why, for example, can we say *I like playing football* and *I like
to play football*, but not **I enjoy to play football*? Or **I want playing
football*?

First of all, let's look at some common patterns using either the *to*-
infinitive, or the *-ing* form (see **38**), or both:

1   *to*-infinitive only: *want, wish, hope, intend*: *I want <u>to play</u> football*.
2   *-ing* form only: *enjoy, dislike, miss, can't help*: *I enjoy <u>playing</u>
    football. I miss <u>playing</u> football*.
3   *to*-infinitive and *-ing* form (although with some difference of
    meaning): *like, love, prefer, remember, forget, begin, start, try*: *I like
    <u>to play / playing</u> football; I started <u>to play / playing</u> football*.

There are at least three possible, overlapping meanings for these patterns:

1   The *to*-infinitive describes a potential, e.g. imagined, situation, often
    in the future, and *to* symbolizes movement towards it. e.g. *I would
    like <u>to play</u> football. I remembered <u>to lock</u> the door*. The *-ing* form,
    on the other hand, expresses real or factual situations: *I enjoy
    <u>playing</u> football. I remember <u>locking</u> the door*.
2   The *to*-infinitive envisages the situation in its entirety, while the
    -ing form sees it as unfolding, in progress: *Would you prefer <u>to sit</u>
    in the front? What do you prefer: <u>playing</u> football or <u>watching</u> it?*
3   The *to*-infinitive is more verb-like and less definite, while the *-ing*
    form is more **noun**-like and more definite: *I like <u>to ski</u>* v *I like <u>skiing</u>*.
    The former implies I do it, whereas the latter might mean I simply
    like watching other people doing it.

In the end, it may not be possible to find a single explanation for all cases.

Does English have gerunds? 40

'Modern grammars do not use the term *gerund*'
(Crystal, 1996). Why not?

Grammarians, trained in the classics, attempted to import the term gerund into English, but with mixed results. In 1965, F.R. Palmer had doubts:

> In many cases it [is] difficult to decide, especially in the case of the *-ing* form, whether it is a nominal [i.e. **noun**-like] or an adjectival [i.e. **adjective**-like], and in fact the traditional grammars have fallen into great difficulties in talking sometimes about '**participles**' and sometimes about 'gerunds'.

What are these 'great difficulties'? Take the word *painting*, for example: when is it **verb**-like, adjective-like, or noun-like? Here are some examples in order from verb-like to noun-like, by way of adjectives:

1 *The images evolve as I'm painting.*
2 *If you ever watched him painting he was very physical.*
3 *By painting fast, their work 'redefined' landscape painting.*
4 *My biggest love is painting outdoors.*
5 *She was supporting herself entirely by painting.*
6 *Wood's painting technique is somewhat unusual.*
7 *Enroll in a pottery or painting class, or have your portrait painted.*
8 *I pursue my painting of landscapes outside of my regular job.*
9 *A painting is, after all, two-dimensional.*

Which of the above are gerunds? If it seems difficult to draw the line, it's because there is a spectrum from 'verbiness' to 'nouniness' that is shared by most *-ing* forms. This is why grammarians now prefer to call them just that: *-ing* forms (see 38).

Crystal, D. (1996) *Rediscover Grammar*. Harlow: Longman.

Palmer, F.R. (1965) *A Linguistic Study of the English Verb*. London: Longmans.

41 What does *do* do?

> Of all the words in English, the one that perhaps causes learners most grief is the auxiliary verb *do*.

Like all **auxiliary verbs** (see **37**) *do*, and its inflected forms *doing, does, did, done*, started life as a lexical **verb**, a function it still retains:

> I <u>do</u> the laundry and they put it away.
> What have you <u>done</u> for me lately?

At some point around 1500, *do* morphed into serving a purely grammatical function, taking the place of the main verb in questions and negatives. Up until then, questions were formed by inverting the **subject** and verb, and negatives were formed by adding *not* to the verb, as in these examples from Shakespeare:

> <u>Know you</u> this ring?   His face I <u>know not</u>.

Shakespeare himself was familiar with the new auxiliary:

> I <u>do not know</u>, my lord, what I should think.

Around about this time, the rules of question formation and negation were being reformulated in these terms:

1   To make a question, invert the subject and first auxiliary: <u>Can you</u> love this lady? <u>Will you</u> go see her?
2   To negate a statement, add *not* to the first auxiliary: She <u>should not</u> visit you. You <u>must not</u> speak of that.

But what if there is no auxiliary to invert or to add *not* to? In the absence of an auxiliary, *do* (and *does* and *did*) were enlisted to perform these functions. Consequently it is sometimes called the *dummy* auxiliary.

Do also substitutes for whole **clauses**: *What, go you toward the Tower? ~I <u>do</u>, my lord.* And it adds emphasis in affirmative **clauses**: *I <u>do</u> fear it.* And it is used in negative **imperatives**: <u>*Do*</u> *not say so, my lord.*

> **For many learners, phrasal verbs have iconic status. Why? What's so special about them?**

A **phrasal verb** is commonly defined as being a multi-word **verb** that consists of a lexical verb and one or more **particles**. Some grammars restrict the term phrasal verb only to verb + **adverb particle** combinations, such as *look up* (= consult), *take back* (= retrieve). Accordingly, verb + **preposition** particles are called prepositional verbs: *look for* (= search), *take after* (= resemble).

So, when is a particle an adverb, and when is it a preposition? Simply, an adverb can stand alone; a preposition needs a **noun complement**:

1 *Look up!* = adverb   2   *Look up the chimney.* = preposition
3 *Look up the word.* = adverb

Up is an adverb in (3) because we can separate it from *look* so that it stands on its own. which is not possible with (2):

4 *Look the word up.*   5   **Look the chimney up.*

Separability, then, is a defining feature of phrasal verbs that take objects: *Look the word up*. *Up the chimney* is simply a prepositional phrase. But we still need to distinguish such phrases from prepositional verbs.

6 *He ran after the bus*. = prepositional phrase
7 *He takes after his father.* = prepositional verb

In (7) there is a stronger connection between *take* and *after* than *run* and *after*. Compare: *After the bus he ran. *After his father he takes.*

Some grammars define phrasal verbs as only those that have idiomatic meaning. But what, then, is idiomatic?

 8 *He wrote down my address.* = not idiomatic?
 9 *He wrote up the lecture.* = idiomatic?
10 *He wrote off the damage.* = idiomatic

Is it any wonder then that phrasal verbs have such iconic status?

43 How many conditionals are there?

> Conditionals express the way one event is dependent upon another, and whether real or imagined.

Unlike some languages, English has no conditional verb form. Instead, we use the **modal verb** *would*: *I would like …*

What English does have are **conditional clauses**: typically they begin with *if … .* The *if*-clause states a condition, on which the main **clause** depends.

1 *If you go to bed at eight, then you'll wake up like six.*
2 *People would miss you if you weren't there.*
3 *I would have been happier if we had won.*

Conditional clauses are often grouped into three types:

- first conditional: *if* + present simple + *will* – as in (1) above.
- second conditional: *if* + past simple + *would* – as in (2) above.
- third conditional: *if* + past perfect + *would have* – as in (3) above.

A fourth type, called the *zero conditional*, accounts for sentences where both verbs are in the present and which state general truths: *If you work very hard, you get to the top.*

But this classification does not cover all the combinations possible. Sometimes these are lumped together under the heading *mixed conditionals*.

I will call you if we are not going to make it. = will + if + going to
It's very tough to get started if you haven't been working. = present simple + if + present perfect

An alternative way of categorizing conditional clauses is simply to distinguish between real and unreal (or hypothetical) conditions. In the case of unreal conditions, the tense of the conditional clause shifts back (see **87**) to indicate an unlikely or impossible situation:

If you wanted something, you had to pay for it. = no backshift: real
If I'd wanted that I would have asked for it. = backshift: unreal

Or is *have gone* a form of the infinitive?

The issue here is: what are the elements of a **verb phrase**, and what is the order in which they are sequenced? These are:

subject	(modal)	(perfect) have/has/ had	(progressive) be/been/is/ was, etc.	(passive) be, etc.	main verb
she					follows
			is	being	followed
		has	been		following
	may	have		been	followed

The table will generate all possible combinations of **tense, aspect, modality** and **voice**, some of which are vanishingly rare – e.g. *she may have been being followed* – and only a few of which have a label (past simple, present perfect, etc).

The combinations with **modal verbs** (*can, could, may*, etc. – see **58**) are always followed by a verb in the **infinitive** form: *can <u>do</u>, may <u>be</u>*, etc. This can either be the present infinitive, or what is called the perfect infinitive: *could <u>go</u>, could <u>have gone</u>*, respectively.

The combination of modal and perfect infinitive resembles the present perfect (see **51**) in having an **auxiliary** *have* plus a past **participle**: *he has <u>gone</u>*, but does not share the same 'meaning space'. *He could have gone home*, for example, can – like the present perfect – refer to an indefinite time in the past, as in *It's possible he has gone home*, or it could refer to a definite time: *He could have gone home after lunch*, which is not possible with the present perfect: **He has gone home after lunch.*

Here are some more examples of modal + perfect infinitive combinations from the Cambridge English Corpus:

You <u>should have been</u> there to see it.
What <u>would it have cost</u> you to tell her how you feel?
It <u>can't have been</u> less than two hours later that I woke up.

D: Verbs – tense and aspect

Continuing the theme of verbs, the next set of questions is concerned with tense and aspect, and the way they combine. This is an area of pedagogical grammar that generates possibly more questions than any other, partly because of the way verb tenses are prioritized on teaching syllabuses, but also because the concepts of tense and aspect are often conflated and hence confused.

45 How many tenses are there?
46 Is the past tense just about past time?
47 How do we talk about the future?
48 Is it *I don't have one* or *I haven't one*?
49 What tense is *have* got?
50 What does *aspect* mean?
51 Why is the present perfect called the *present perfect*?
52 When do you use the past, and when the present perfect?
53 *She's gone to Peru* or *She's been to Peru*?
54 What is progressive about the present progressive?
55 Is *I am loving it* wrong?
56 What's the difference between *I've been working* and *I've worked*?
57 When do we use the past perfect?

How many tenses are there?

> **3? 12? 16? 36? The answer depends on how you define 'tense'.**

Grammatical **tense** is the way **verbs** are marked (or **inflected**) to express a relation with time. In English, there is a two-way contrast between present and past tense: *they work/they worked; I see/I saw.* From a strictly formal perspective, then, there are only two tenses.

Of course, we experience time as having past, present and future. It would be logical to think that grammatical tense neatly maps on to our experience. It doesn't. We can use past tense to talk about the present (*It's time you <u>went</u> to bed*) and present tense to talk about the past (*1812: Napoleon <u>invades</u> Russia*). And we can use both to talk about the future: *Your bus <u>leaves</u> at seven this evening. I wish you <u>weren't</u> working tomorrow.*

Put simply, there is no one-to-one match between (grammatical) tense and (notional) time. Nevertheless, present tense verbs correlate strongly with present time (although not necessarily the time of speaking) and past tense verbs most commonly have past reference.

Tense combines with **aspect** (see **50**) to create the variety of verb structures in English that are commonly, if mistakenly, known as its different *tenses.* These are:

	no aspect (simple)	perfect	progressive	perfect + progressive
present	*they work*	*they have worked*	*they are working*	*they have been working*
past	*they worked*	*they had worked*	*they were working*	*they had been working*

The number of these so-called tenses can be increased even more if we add **voice** (**passive** and active) and create a category in the table above for the future (see **47**).

46   Is the past tense just about past time?

> A significant number of past forms have present or future
> time orientation. How is this possible?

The point has been made (see **45**) that notional time and grammatical
tense don't always match. A good example of this is the way that, in
English, the past tense is used to express unreal or hypothetical meaning
with reference to the present or future, as in these examples:

> *I worry what we would do if we <u>had</u> a really bad accident.*
> *She wishes she <u>was</u> back at work.*
> *What if you <u>got</u> laid off tomorrow?*
> *I think it's time you <u>were</u> upstairs and in bed.*

Less frequently, the past tense with present meaning is used as a marker
of politeness, as in these **corpus** examples:

> *Angela, <u>did</u> you want some of the raspberry too? ~ Yes please.*
> *I <u>was</u> wondering if you could spare any change.*
> *Sorry, what <u>was</u> the name again? ~ Liz.*
> *<u>Did</u> you want to go first, then?*

These alternative uses of the past tense have led some grammarians to
argue that there is a core meaning that all past tense uses share, and
that is *distance* or *remoteness*. According to this view, the present tense
(which they call the non-remote tense) expresses presence or actuality,
whereas the past (the remote tense) expresses absence or unreality. So,
an event can be remote in time, as in *Shakespeare was born in Stratford.*
Or it can be remote in terms of reality, as in *If I was Shakespeare … .*
Or it can be remote in terms of social distance: *I wanted to ask you … .*

The non-remote/remote distinction helps explain why we can use the
present (i.e. non-remote) tense to talk about past events, in order to
make them seem immediate, as in:

> *This guy <u>walks</u> into a bar ….*
> *As Shakespeare <u>says</u> ….*
> *PRIME MINISTER <u>RESIGNS</u>!*

How do we talk about the future? 47

If there's no future tense, how do we talk about the future?

If we define (grammatical) **tense** as being the way that the **verb** system indicates time relations, then English is seriously limited: there are only two ways that tense is marked – with or without *-ed* (in regular verbs): *I work, I worked.* (see **45**). Unlike many languages, e.g. Italian or Portuguese, there is no future tense **inflection**.

Instead, there are a number of different ways that futurity can be expressed, principally through the use of **aspect** and **modality**.

- **modal verb** *will* + **infinitive** (sometimes called the future simple): *I will be sixty this year.* This is by far the most common way of expressing the future in English, and is the nearest thing to a 'future tense'.

- *going to* + infinitive: This expresses the future as in some sense connected to the present, either because of a present intention: *Now they are going to get married;* or as a prediction based on present evidence: *I think it's going to snow.*

(For the difference between *will* and *going to*, see **62**.)

- present simple: This is used mainly to talk about scheduled events: *School starts in two weeks.* Or in **subordinate clauses** (see **63**): *What will they find when they get here?*

- present progressive: This is used mainly to talk about arrangements: *My father is coming over for Christmas.*

- *will* + *be* + *-ing* (the future progressive): to talk about plans and arrangements: *They'll be meeting later with the president.* And to talk about future events that are seen as happening as a matter of course: *We will be landing in ten minutes.*

- *will* + *have* + *-ed* (the future perfect): This expresses a future event seen as completed, looking back from another point in the future: *By June we'll have had a successful season.*

48 Is it *I don't have one* or *I haven't one*?

> Or how do you negate a lexical verb that is also an auxiliary verb?

Have is both a lexical **verb** (with the basic meaning of 'possess') and an **auxiliary verb** (see 37). Lexical verbs are negated by adding *not* (or its contracted form *n't*) to the first auxiliary that is present:

1 You <u>can't</u> have any food on you.

Or, in the absence of an auxiliary, by inserting the dummy auxiliary *do* (see **41**) and adding *not*:

2 We <u>don't</u> have a lot of money.

To form the negative of *have* as an auxiliary verb, on the other hand, simply add *not*:

3 Has he done his homework? → <u>Hasn't</u> he done his homework?

What can be confusing is that this auxiliary-like construction can also be used with the lexical verb *have*, and always with *have got* (see **49**):

4 She <u>hasn't</u> a clue what they are on about.
5 'I <u>haven't got</u> the foggiest idea,' he said.

There is a third pattern of negation with *have*, which is to use *no* with the following noun, as in:

6 I have <u>no clue</u> why this should be so.
7 The Jenkins house had <u>no hot running water</u>.

Biber et al (1999) have shown in their **corpus** data that this is the most common pattern with indefinite **objects** (*no clue, no place*), whereas *not*-negation with *do* is the most common with definite objects, e.g. *I don't have <u>the time</u>*. Auxiliary-like *not*-negation (as in example 4), on the other hand, is relatively uncommon, apart from in fiction.

Biber D., Johansson, S., Leech, G., Conrad, S. and Finegan, E. (1999) *Longman Grammar of Spoken and Written English*. Harlow: Longman.

I've got a dog and *I have a dog* seem synonymous. But their negative forms are very different: *I haven't got a dog* and *I don't have a dog*. So are they the same tense?

Like its counterpart *have* (see **48**), *have got* can be a lexical **verb** meaning possession: *I've got a new phone*, or a **modal**-like verb meaning obligation: *I've got to rush*, or certainty: *You've got to be joking!* (see **60**).

Have got dates back to the 16th century and, as its form suggests, started life as a present perfect construction: the **auxiliary verb** *have* plus the past **participle** of *get*, meaning something like *to have acquired, taken* or *received*, as in Shakespeare: *The army of the queen hath got the field.* (*Henry VI Part III*) This sense is retained in US English: *What response have you gotten to the book? He's gotten similar results using humans.*

Condemned by grammar purists in the 19th century, *have got* is now firmly established, in all its senses, particularly in British English. However, *have* is still preferred in some contexts, such as when making statements of a general or habitual, rather than specific, character:

> *Do most people have television?* v *I've got a TV and a stereo player.*
> *We often have visitors from abroad.* v *Leslie's got a visitor with him.*

Also, *have got* is less common in the past:

> *I had back trouble, and so I had one of those inflatable balls.*
> *We had to feed them, we had to look after them.*

The tendency to reduce *have got* to *got* is characteristic of informal, particularly US, English: *I'm like 'Do whatever you got to do'.*

In similar contexts, *got to* is spelled *gotta* to represent the weak form of *to*, as in *She's Gotta Have It* (a film by Spike Lee). Indeed, like *gonna*, *gotta* is a good example of how a lexical word becomes fully grammaticised over time.

50   **What does *aspect* mean?**

> *Aspect* means *a way of looking at something*. Grammatical aspect conveys the way that situations look.

There are two grammatical **aspects** in English: the progressive (also called continuous) and the perfect. Both aspects are formed by a combination of **auxiliary verbs** and **participles**. The auxiliary verbs can be marked for **tense**, and the two aspects can be combined. (See **45**.)

Very generally, adding progressive aspect conveys a meaning of 'in progress' (see **54**):

1   *She <u>worked</u> in Athens.* → *She <u>was working</u> in Athens.*

Adding perfect aspect conveys a meaning of retrospection (see **51**):

2   *She <u>works</u> in Athens.* → *She <u>has worked</u> in Athens.*

Note that in each of the paired sentences in (1) and (2) the **tense** is the same: past and present respectively.

Depending on the context and the meaning of the verb (its **lexical aspect**), a range of secondary meanings are possible. For example, if a verb is a **stative verb**, i.e. if it usually describes a permanent state, adding progressive aspect can turn it into a temporary behaviour:

3   *She <u>is</u> unreasonable.* → *She <u>is being</u> unreasonable.*

If a verb describes a single momentary action, adding progressive implies repetition:

4   *Someone <u>shouted</u>.* → *Someone <u>was shouting</u>.*

Depending on associated time expressions, perfect aspect can imply a situation that is complete or incomplete:

5   *She has worked in Athens <u>before</u>.* v *She has worked in Athens <u>for years</u>.*

But in both cases the situation is seen retrospectively from the present.

Why is the present perfect called the *present* perfect?

51

> Think of the present perfect as having one foot in the past and one foot in the present.

Here are some fairly typical examples of the present perfect:

1 *We've been friends since college.*
2 *The* Eagle *has landed.*
3 *I've just had breakfast.*

In each case the **auxiliary verb** *have* is in the present **tense**. This is because the present perfect is a present tense too. But it has an added element of **aspect** (see **50**). The aspectual meaning of the perfect is one of viewing the past from the perspective of the present. So, the combination of present tense and perfect aspect expresses a connection to the present, even though the situation may have started in the past. So, in (1) we are still friends. In (2) the *Eagle* is still where it landed, and in (3) I had breakfast so recently that the effects are still present.

But in this sentence the events started and finished in the past:

4 *She's been to Korea – twice.*

What is present about that? The point is that her visits to Korea happened in a time period that began in the past and extends to the present, with the implication that the experience has some present relevance. For example, it might be part of an exchange like:

What's Seoul like? ~ Ask Joan. She's been to Korea – twice.

In this case, the past - present connection is less temporal than notional: the past experience is seen as having present relevance.

The linguist Otto Jespersen put his finger on it nearly a century ago: 'The Perfect is a retrospective present, which connects a past occurrence with the present time, either as continued up to the present moment ... or as having results or consequences bearing on the present moment'.

Jespersen, O. (1933) *Essentials of English Grammar.* London: Allen & Unwin

52 When do you use the past, and when the present perfect?

English makes a distinction between events that are seen as in some way connected to present time and those that are not. For disconnected events, the past tense is preferred.

The following (authentic) learner errors are very common:

1 *Where <u>have you been</u> last night? You said you'd stay home.* (= *were you*)
2 *You won't believe what <u>has happened</u> at my school yesterday.* (= *happened*)
3 *How are you since the last time we<u>'ve seen</u> each other?* (= *saw*)
4 *<u>Have you been</u> shopping yesterday? What clothes <u>have you bought</u>?* (= *Did you go/did you buy*)
5 *I <u>lived</u> here since I was born.* (= *have lived*)
6 *How are you? I <u>didn't see</u> you for 2 weeks.* (= *haven't seen*)
7 *That would be nice for me too, because I never <u>went</u> to England yet.* (= *have never been*)
8 *My mother and brother are here with me. We already <u>went</u> to the sea and it was beautiful.* (= *have already been*)

The main cause of difficulty is in not distinguishing between events that are disconnected from the present (examples 1–4), and those that are in some way connected to it (examples 5–8; see 51).

Examples 1–4 explicitly place the events in a definite time in the past: *last night, yesterday, the last time.* Even when the time is not mentioned, it is often implied: *That's a nice dress. Where <u>did you buy</u> it?*

Examples 5–8, on the other hand, are connected to the present, because the time period extends to and includes the present: *since I was born, for 2 weeks, never ... yet* (i.e. in all my life up to now), *already* (because *already* indicates that the event has happened sooner than expected in the period leading up to the present).

She's gone to Peru or She's been to Peru?

What is the present perfect of *go*: *She's gone to Peru* or *She's been to Peru*?

Some grammar books give two past participles for the **verb** *to go*: *gone* and *been*. This is because *gone to* implies going, whereas *been to* implies both going and returning. Compare these two (invented) exchanges, for example:

> *How's Jill? ~ She's gone to Peru.*
> *Oh. When does she get back? ~ Next week.*

> *How's Jill? ~ She's been to Peru.*
> *Oh. When did she get back? ~ Last week.*

Notice that the distinction isn't maintained in the past simple, where *She went to Peru last year* could mean that she went and stayed, or that she went and came back.

Learners commonly overuse *gone* (*to*), producing sentences that while technically accurate, don't sound completely idiomatic, as in these learner examples from the Cambridge English Corpus:

> *I have <u>gone</u> to foreign countries many times and I know the problems of being in a foreign country.*
> *It was Sunday evening and I was very tired because I had <u>gone</u> out all the day with my friends.*
> *This park is the best I've ever <u>gone</u> to, because it's so calm.*
> *If you have never <u>gone</u> to a concert, I really think it's time to start.*

All of these examples would be improved by using *been*, not *gone*.

There are many fewer examples of the misuse of *been to*, but here is one:

> *As my boss has <u>been</u> to Prague for a business conference, I can not leave my office.*

54 What is progressive about the present progressive?

Or, what is continuous about the present continuous?

The progressive (also called *continuous*) is one of the two **verb aspects** in English (see 50). The other is the perfect (see 51). The progressive is formed from the **auxiliary verb** *be* and the *-ing* form (see 38): *Big Brother is watching you. The Russians are coming.*

The progressive combines with **tense** to form a variety of structures such as the present progressive, past progressive and future progressive. It also combines with the perfect to form the present and past perfect progressive (see 45 for a table displaying these forms). It can also combine with modal auxiliaries: *The plane will be landing soon. You must be joking.*

The progressive is not a tense, so it doesn't tell us *when* an action happened so much as what the action *was like*. The basic meaning of the progressive is (as its name implies) that the event or situation is viewed as being 'in progress' (in the present or the past, depending on the context). According to the context, and to the type of verb (i.e. its **lexical aspect**), this can have secondary implications, such as that the situation is not finished, that it is temporary, or that it is repeated.

Pedagogical grammars insist that the present progressive is used to talk about activities happening at the moment of speaking: *I'm just getting on the train.* While this is true in many instances, it doesn't account for the following **corpus** examples. What they all have in common, however, is the idea of an activity being in progress at some time:

> *I'm meeting Laura for Thai food in half an hour.*
> *One day he's riding his bike to work in Jakarta; the next he's in Manhattan.*
> *Every time I talk to him he's going through the food line.*
> *Suddenly, this guy is walking toward me, sort of shuffling along.*
> *We're always looking for the next big trend in food.*
> *When I'm having a bad day, I just think of Toon.*

Is *I am loving it* wrong? 55

This phrase is perplexing: isn't it wrong to use *love* in the progressive form?

Verbs are divided into different classes, according to **lexical aspect** (see **50**). A basic distinction is made between **stative verbs** (also known as state verbs) and dynamic (or action) verbs. Stative verbs are divided into:

- relational verbs: *be, belong, consist of, fit, have, include, own, resemble, seem, sound,* etc.
- verbs of cognition: *believe, know, remember, think, understand,* etc.
- sensory verbs: *feel, hear, see, smell, taste*
- verbs of emotions: *desire, dislike, like, love, prefer, want, wish,* etc.

Because these verbs describe states rather than processes, they are not often used with progressive aspect (see **54**). This is because the progressive highlights the dynamic nature of verbs: *The boys were pushing each other.* But not **The boys were resembling each other.*

Some of these verbs, however, can be used with the progressive when they describe an activity in progress and have an agent:

> *The soup tastes good.* v *I've been tasting the soup.*
> *I think it might rain.* v *I'm thinking of getting a cat.*
> *Do you have a pen?* v *Are you having a bath?*

Similarly, some stative verbs that are not normally used in the progressive are occurring in this form with increasing frequency.

> *I'm feeling more like I'm understanding this country, this society.*
> *She's got a real job, and she's loving it.*
> *I could feel no one was believing me.*
> *The delay is costing us a lot of money.*

The effect of adding progressive aspect to state verbs is to turn them into dynamic verbs – to turn a state into an action or process that has stages and unfolds over time.

56 What's the difference between *I've been working* and *I've worked*?

That is to say, what's the difference between the present perfect simple and the present perfect progressive? Is it about being finished v unfinished? Or is it about permanent v temporary activities?

One of the problems of comparing any two structures like this is the lack of context. Questions such as finished v unfinished, or permanent v temporary, can't be resolved without looking at the larger picture. Compare, for example, these two real occurrences from the Cambridge English Corpus:

1   *Ms. Garcia, 61, has worked as an independent education consultant since 2001.*
2   *I will never reach the success that my dad has felt. He's 50 years old and he's been working in the business for 28 years.*

It's clear from the context that both situations are unfinished and *not* temporary. In the next examples, however, at least some of the work referred to is presumably finished, and probably temporary:

3   *Deidre Prince has worked with some of Hollywood's most vivacious leading men.*
4   *Hayes has been working off and on in Iowa since October and returned here Wednesday.*

If there is any difference in meaning, it is not about the time. All four examples are in the present **tense**, with perfect **aspect** indicating that the events are viewed looking back from the time of speaking (see **51**). It is the contribution of progressive aspect that makes the difference to (2) and (4): adding *-ing* to a verb like *work* has the effect of emphasizing its dynamic, unfolding, 'in progress' quality (see **54**). Depending on the **verb**, this can have different effects:

5   *Have you seen my mother?*
6   *Have you been seeing my mother?*

When do we use the past perfect? 57

> One of the main functions of the past perfect is to provide background information.

The past perfect (e.g. *the train had left*) combines the past **tense** (*had*) and perfect **aspect** in order to look back from a point already in the past. The viewpoint (underlined in the following examples) may be made explicit in an **adverbial clause** of time:

> *The train had already left Sion <u>when the avalanche struck</u>.*
> *Skidmore had written six novels <u>by the time he was 30</u>.*

Or it may be indicated by a reporting verb in the past:

> *Kathleen <u>said</u> it had been a tough week for the family.*

Or the viewpoint may be the start of a narrative:

> *We had been out for one of our evening rambles, Holmes and I, and had returned about six o'clock on a cold, frosty winter's evening. As Holmes turned up the lamp <u>the light fell upon a card on the table</u>.*

> (From Arthur Conan Doyle's *The Return of Sherlock Holmes*.)

The past perfect often explains why past events occurred:

> *Everywhere on their journey through France they found the people mad with celebration, for the king <u>had agreed</u> to observe the new constitution.*

The past perfect can also be used to give background information in **relative clauses**:

> *Angry e-mails poured in to the woman who <u>had imposed</u> the new rules.*

The past perfect is only necessary if the sequence of events is not obvious. In these sentences, the sequence is obvious: *After she sang, she sat*. But not: **When she sang, she sat*.

E: Verbs – modality and voice

Not only are verbs marked for tense and aspect, but, by means of modality, they express shades of meaning associated with the speaker's (or writer's) stance, that is to say their judgement as to the likelihood or desirability of a proposition. And, through the use of voice, i.e. the choice between active and passive, they also reflect the way that the information in an utterance can be organized so as to distinguish new from given information, for example.

> **Modal verbs are the commonest grammatical means of expressing attitude.**

Modal verbs are a kind of **auxiliary** (or 'helping') **verb** (see **37**). There are nine 'pure' modals: *will, would, shall, should, can, could, may, might* and *must*.

They are pure in the sense that they fulfil the formal requirements of auxiliary verbs:

1 They form negatives with *not/n't*: *She cannot go; Kim wouldn't do it.*
2 They form questions by inversion with their **subject**: *Can she go? Would Kim do it?*
3 They do not have **infinitive** forms, **participles** or third person -*s*.

If there are other auxiliaries in the verb **phrase**, modals are always placed before them: *It may have been damaged.*

Each modal verb can express two kinds of meaning: (1) *logical meaning*, which includes likelihood, possibility, and futurity; and (2) *personal meaning*, i.e. a range of meanings to do with wishes, intentions, obligations, etc. In the absence of context, it's not always clear which of these two meanings is being expressed. For example, *She may go* can mean both *She is likely to go*, and *She is allowed to go.*

Each modal, apart from *must* (see **66**), forms a pair with similar meanings: *will/would; shall/should*, etc. The second of each pair can have past tense meaning, especially in reported contexts: *Will it rain? She asked if it would rain.* All the modals (but *can* only in the negative) combine with the perfect infinitive (*have done* etc.) to express a more restricted range of past meanings (see **44**). *She may have gone*, for example, is a statement about likelihood, not permission.

Because of their wide range of meanings, modals allow speakers to express a variety of functions, e.g. asking permission, making requests, giving advice and making offers. They also express a variety of notions, such as obligation, necessity, ability, futurity and possibility.

> 'Can I go to the restroom, miss?' 'You *can*, but you *may*
> not.' How many of us have experienced that exchange?

Can is the third most common **modal auxiliary** (see **58**), outranked only
by *will* and *would*. Its core meaning is something like 'to be able to, or
free to, do something', a meaning shared by its three main uses:

1 to talk about one's ability or inability to do something:

   If you <u>can</u> walk, you <u>can</u> dance; if you <u>can</u> talk, you <u>can</u> sing.
   I <u>can't</u> even vaguely afford it.

2 to request, give, or refuse permission

   <u>Can</u> I go to lunch now? ~ You <u>can</u> do what you want.
   I'm sorry but you <u>can't</u> live here.

3 to talk about what sometimes happens, i.e. a theoretical possibility

   Soccer isn't an extreme sport but it <u>can</u> be quite exhilarating.
   In May it <u>can</u> get up to about at least a hundred degrees.

Notice that requesting permission is listed as a function of *can*. In
fact, along with *could,* it is by far the most common way of asking
permission: *may* is relatively infrequent, and used more to talk about
possibility than permission: *I suspect you may be a lawyer.*

To talk about the past, *could* is used in all the same senses as *can,*
although with certain limitations:

1 to talk about general abilities or theoretical possibilities in the past:
   *A hadrosaur <u>could</u> run faster than a T. rex; it looked like it <u>could</u> get
   really nasty.* But not for specific achievements: *One of our bikes had a
   flat tyre, but we <u>were able to</u> change it.* (Not *we could change it.*)
2 when reporting permission: *I asked if we <u>could</u> have the TV on.*

Are *ought to* and *have to* modal verbs? 60

> *Ought to* and *have to* don't feature in the list of 'pure' modals, yet they clearly have modal meaning.

The nine 'pure modals' (see **58**) are defined in terms of how they form negatives and questions, and how they combine with the bare **infinitive** of lexical **verbs** to construct verb **phrases**. They also share the characteristic of having both logical and personal meaning. *Ought to* fulfils all these criteria, except for the presence of *to*. Compare *You should see a doctor* and *You ought to see a doctor*. *Ought to* is also less common than its nearest equivalent *should*, and seldom occurs in negative or question forms. Nevertheless, it has both logical and personal meaning, as these **corpus** examples show:

> *When one hears Dutch one feels one <u>ought to</u> be able understand it.* (= logical meaning)
> *You really <u>ought to</u> discuss this with him.* (= personal meaning)

Other so-called 'marginal modals' are *need* and *dare*, which sometimes behave like modal **auxiliaries**, and sometimes like lexical verbs:

> *You <u>needn't</u> worry.* (auxiliary-like)
> *You <u>don't need to</u> worry.* (verb-like)
> *<u>Do you need to</u> think about it?* (verb-like)

> *<u>Don't you dare</u> speak to my friend like that!* (verb-like)
> *She <u>didn't dare to</u> ask.* (verb-like)
> *She <u>dared not</u> ask.* (auxiliary-like, but less common)

There are also a number of modal phrases that have modal meaning and often have a near equivalent among the 'pure' modal auxiliaries. For example: *have (got) to*; *be able to*; *be going to*; *used to*.

Does *used to* have a present tense?

> *Used to* is used to talk about past habits. What about present habits?

Used to is a **modal**-like construction (see **60**) that refers to discontinued past habits and states, as in these **corpus** examples:

1   We <u>used to</u> spend summers in the Lake District.
2   He seemed charming at first. He <u>used to</u> take her to dances.
3   'It's gotten so bad,' she said. 'It <u>didn't use to</u> be this way.'
4   <u>Didn't there use to</u> be a cottage where them big tanks is?

As such, *used to* has no present **tense**: to talk about present habits and states there are a number of possibilities:

We usually eat in. = present simple with **adverb** of frequency

On a typical day I'll wake up at 5am. = *will* for predictable behaviour

Learners sometimes confuse *used to* (for past habits) with *to be/get used to*, meaning 'to/get become accustomed to', which can be used in the present as well as the past. Note that here *to* is a **preposition** so it is followed by a **noun** or an *-ing* form, not an **infinitive**:

> It takes time for teachers and students to <u>get used to</u> the tests.
> People in Montana <u>weren't used to</u> seeing Asians.

Used to (for past habits) has a related **modal verb**, *would*. The main difference is that, while *used to* can be used both for events (examples 1 and 2 above) and states (3 and 4), *would* is normally only used to talk about past events – often a chain of events in sequence:

> We <u>would</u> meet so once a week and I <u>would</u> erm present the topic to both the professor and the other MPhil students.

There is also the **verb** *to use*, of course, the past of which is *used* – but pronounced /juːzd/, not /juːst/: *Tear gas was <u>used</u> to break up the demonstration.*

What's the difference between *going to* and *will*?

> Although, strictly speaking, there's no future tense in English, *will* and *going to* might be candidates for the position. So, what's the difference?

Like all **modals** (see **58**) and most modal **phrases** (see **60**), *will* and *going to* each express two kinds of meaning: logical meaning and personal meaning:

modal	modal meaning	notion	example
will	logical	prediction	*They say it <u>will</u> drive away business.*
	personal	willingness	*Don't worry, we'<u>ll</u> look after her.*
going to	logical	prediction	*The price of corn is <u>going to</u> rise.*
	personal	intention	*I'm not <u>going to</u> say anything.*

In other words, there's a lot of overlap between the two forms, and, particularly with regard to prediction, they are often interchangeable:

> *Do you think it'<u>s going to</u> get worse or do you think it <u>will</u> get better?*

If there is any difference, it is attributable to the fact that *going to* is a present tense form (it started life as the present progressive) and hence implies a strong connection to the present. The connection associated with prediction is that there is present evidence: *Early indicators suggest it's <u>going to</u> be hot.* (But *it will be hot* is feasible here too.)

The connection associated with intention is that the decision has already been made: *I don't care what people think. I'<u>m going to</u> get married.* (Here *I'll get married* is less likely, unless *will* is stressed).

Because *will* is associated with willingness (see **65**), it is often used to make offers, promises and threats, especially if the decision co-occurs with the utterance: *Come inside. I'<u>ll</u> make us some coffee.*

There are also register differences: while *will* is more common overall, *going to* is much more common in conversation.

I'll call when I arrive: why not when I will arrive?

> If my arrival is in the future, why don't I use a future form?

The rule, put simply, states that, when the main **clause** has future reference, the **adverbial** clause of time (i.e. a clause starting with *when, as soon as, until,* etc.) is in the present **tense** – as in these examples:

> *I'll call you when I <u>get</u> to Ashfield.* (Not **when I will get to Ashfield*)
> *But what will happen when she <u>marries</u>?*
> *As soon as we <u>know</u> it, we'll let you know.*
> *Will you be able to handle things here until Mr. Waverly <u>gets</u> back?*

The same tense simplification is used in **conditional clauses**:

> *What will they do if it <u>rains</u>?* (Not **if it will rain*)
> *They won't be proud of me if I <u>tell</u> them.*

and with other present tenses, such as the present perfect:

> *She will have to wait until I <u>have finished</u>.* (Not **until I will have finished*)

The reason this happens is that the **subordinate clause** establishes a background, stretching from the present moment, against which the main event occurs or might occur. This is why the present tense in these kinds of clauses is sometimes called *the background future*.

Sometimes, **modal** *will* occurs in these clauses, but with the meaning of willingness, rather than prediction:

> *If you <u>will</u> excuse me, I will now take my leave of you.*
> *Well then, if you <u>won't</u> come, we'll carry you off by force!*

Learners often overgeneralize future forms in these structures, as these **corpus** examples show:

> *I will write to you when I <u>will be</u> in Bordeaux.* (= am)
> *When I <u>will have</u> more money I will buy a new stereo.* (= have)

Shall (negative *shan't*) is the least frequent of the pure modals and, in some varieties of English, scarcely exists at all. So, what use is it?

There was a time when *shall* was much more common than it is now. Here, for example, is Jane Austen using it in 1815:

'Dear me! but what <u>shall</u> you do? How <u>shall</u> you employ yourself when you grow old?'

'If I draw less, I <u>shall</u> read more; if I give up music, I <u>shall</u> take to carpet-work.' (*Emma*)

The rules as to when to use *shall* v *will* were extremely opaque: Fowler and Fowler, in *The King's English* (1930) devote 20 pages to the distinction, and happily acknowledge that it 'is so complicated that those who are not to the manner born can hardly acquire it'.

Not surprisingly, perhaps, little attention is now paid to it. *Shall* survives in British English mainly in its personal functions of offering and making – or asking for – suggestions, typically in question form, as in these **corpus** examples:

Okay right yeah <u>shall</u> we break for dinner?
Where <u>shall</u> I sit?
Let's stick with the motion, <u>shall</u> we?

In the first two examples, *should* would be an acceptable alternative in, for example, American English, or *will* in Irish English.

The negative *shan't* is even less common but survives in fiction and in expressions like *I shan't be long*; *I shan't complain*; *I shan't trouble you*.

A formal, legalistic use of *shall* is also retained in contexts where rules or commands are being given:

The decision of the Referee <u>shall</u> be final.
Judicial rules specifically state: 'A judge <u>shall</u> not practise law'.

65 *She won't eat meat*: present or future?

> The modal auxiliary *will/won't* is commonly associated with the future. But does it always refer to the future?

Will comes from the same root as *willing* and the **transitive** English **verb** *to will* – as in *I really think that she willed herself to live*. Although over time *will* evolved into a marker of futurity, it still retains some its original meaning of volition (see **62**). This is the case when it forms part of an offer, request, or refusal, for example:

> *But I'll help him. I'll do everything I can.*
> *Louis Walsh is on the phone, will you talk to him?*
> *I certainly won't be buying any fireworks this year.*

The volitional use of *will* is also common in expressions of politeness: *If you will excuse me … if you will take a seat … .*

While the above cases imply some (imminent) future action, we can use *will/won't* to talk about habitual, i.e. present, acts of (un)willingness:

> *He'll eat fish, but he won't eat meat.*
> *Well if you will go poking around, it's asking for trouble.*
> *Dad has my car … his won't start.*

In the same way, the prediction sense of *will* can be used to talk about predictable behaviour in an extended present:

> *If you live or work near Buckingham Palace, you will occasionally see a Rolls Royce with no number plate.*
> *As long as there are cigarettes, kids will smoke them.*

And *will* can be used to make deductions about present events:

> *[phone rings] I guess that'll be the tea order.*
> *It's only quarter past one, he'll be having his lunch now.*
> *Whoever is out there will have seen our light, and knows we're awake.*

The last two examples demonstrate that all 'future **tenses**' – such as the future progressive and the future perfect – can have present meaning.

Of the nine pure modal auxiliaries, *must* is the only one that does not have a matched past tense form.

Must is what is called a *defective verb*, in the sense that it has no past **tense**. This has not always been the case. Two hundred years ago, the past of *must* was *must*. Here is Jane Austen using it in 1811:

> It was NOT Colonel Brandon – neither his air – nor his height. Were it possible, she <u>must</u> say it <u>must</u> be Edward. (*Sense and Sensibility*)

The past use of *must* survives in some contexts, such as reported speech: *She said I <u>must</u> come to dinner.* But *had to* (the past of *have to* – see **67**) has replaced it, especially in its 'obligation' sense, as in these examples:

> Back then, you <u>had to</u> have a real talent for singing.
> I <u>didn't have to</u> be at my job until noon.

Similarly, *have to* is used with future reference:

> You<u>'ll have to</u> get another set of keys by Tuesday.

Had to is also used, with **state verbs**, to talk about what was considered a strong probability in the past:

> If there was a sea route, it <u>had to</u> be around the bottom of Africa.
> Bush <u>had to</u> know at the time his claims weren't true.

More usually, when making deductions now about past probabilities, *must have + -ed*, and its opposite, *can't have + -ed*, are preferred:

> Someone else <u>must have moved</u> the body.
> Surely such a man <u>can't have made</u> a mistake.

Occasionally, deduction about the past and obligation in the past can be combined in the same clause:

> You <u>must have had to</u> leave Arendale very early this morning.

What is the difference between *you have to* and *you must*?

Both *must* and *have to* refer to obligation. But there are some subtle differences.

Learners frequently confuse *must* and *have to*, with a tendency to overuse the former. For example:

1 *The next week I <u>must</u> do an exam, so I <u>must</u> learn.*
2 *I only go shopping when I <u>must</u> to buy a football ....*
3 *We left your house so quickly because we <u>must</u> go to Cambridge.*
4 *On Sunday when we <u>mustn't</u> work, the shops are closed.*
5 *I'm so happy that you are getting married, you <u>have to</u> be so excited.*

Must expresses an obligation that the speaker imposes ('from within'), while *have (got) to* expresses a duty or regulation that is imposed by a third party ('from without'). So, example (1) would be improved by substituting *have/has to*. And *have to* is preferred where the obligation is a repeated or habitual one, as in the case of (2). Because *must* has no past **tense** (see **66**), *had to* is needed in (3).

The negatives of each form differ even more in terms of meaning: *must not* (*mustn't*) is negative obligation, or prohibition; *don't have to* (or *haven't got to*) is the absence of obligation – the intended meaning in (4), presumably.

Finally, the logical deduction use of *must* is not always generalizable to *have to*, so (5) should be: *you must be so excited.*

Must/mustn't are also overused by learners in contexts where *should/shouldn't* would be less assertive, so more appropriate:

I would like to help you, but you <u>must</u> change your work. (= should)
You <u>mustn't</u> spend your money in useless things. (= shouldn't)

Is *may* the same as *might*?

> If two grammar items are interchangeable, and occur in the
> same contexts, chances are that one of them will become
> 'extinct'. Which is not the case with *may* and *might*.

So, is *might* interchangeable with *may*? In most instances, yes:

1 *It may rain. = It might rain.*
2 *She may have forgotten. = She might have forgotten.*
3 *May I use the printer? = Might I use the printer?*

Some grammars suggest that – when talking about probability – *might*
is less certain than *may*. But both can be intensified in the same way:

4 *It may very well rain. = It might very well rain.*

Likewise, some grammars argue that – when asking permission – *might*
is more tentative. But nowadays even *may* sounds overly polite.

However, in some cases the two are not interchangeable:

- unreal conditions: *If I had the time, I might learn Russian.*
- complaints about failure to do something: *You might have phoned!*
- *might* but not *may* can be used to ask questions about probability:
  Might it rain?
- *might* can't be used to grant permission, like *may*: *You may start
  writing now.*
- likewise, *may not* (= no permission) can't be replaced with *might
  not*: *You may not smoke in here.*
- *may* in the sense of *I wish* is not interchangeable: *May he rest in peace.*

As Downing and Locke argue (2006), 'factors such as speakers' age and
social dialect, and the degree of formality or informality of the situation,
undoubtedly influence the choice of modal. We suggest that *may* is more
formal and indicates reserve, *might* being now the more neutral form'.

Downing A. and Locke, P. (2006) *English Grammar: A University Course*. London:
Routledge.

69 Is there a subjunctive in English?

'Damn the subjunctive,' Mark Twain said (1935). 'It brings all our writers to shame.' It's not clear what Twain's objection was. My question is: is there a subjunctive at all?

The subjunctive is a **verb** form which exists in many languages to express a range of meanings such as uncertainty, wishes and desires. So in French, you might say *Il va falloir que je m'en aille* ('I ought to be going'), where *aille* is the present subjunctive form of *aller*, 'to go'.

It contrasts with the indicative, which is the form of the verb used to describe real states and the **imperative**, which is used to give commands. These are called *grammatical moods*. In English, no subjunctive form survives, apart from *were*, in expressions like *If I were you … .*

What does survive in some varieties (such as American English, and even then, mainly in more formal registers) is the use of the uninflected 'base' form of the verb in some constructions that express suggestions or demands (called *the mandatory subjunctive*). For example:

> *It is very important that he <u>come</u> to Massachusetts, that he <u>come</u> to trial.*
> *It is essential that land <u>be</u> set aside for the animals.*
> *New York state requires that a medical director <u>have</u> emergency medical training.*
> *The officers demanded they not <u>be</u> involved in any such arrests.*

In British English it is more usual to insert *should*, as in *It is essential that land <u>should</u> be set aside for the animals.*

The subjunctive also survives, as has been mentioned, as *were* in past conditional constructions (see **70**), and in some rather old-fashioned formulaic expressions: *So <u>be</u> it. <u>Come</u> what may. God <u>save</u> the Queen.*

Twain, M. (1935) *Mark Twain's Notebook*. New York: Harper and Brothers.

70

> Language is used to talk about unreal as well as real situations. Many languages do this by means of the subjunctive. How do we do it in English?

Since the subjunctive in English has all but disappeared (see **69**), there needs to be another way of signalling non-factual or hypothetical meanings. This is done by the use of what is called *backshift* (see **87**), that is, shifting the **tense** of the **verb** 'back' one: if the unreality is in the present, the verb shifts to the past, e.g.: *I wish I <u>spoke</u> Korean (but I don't)*. If the unreality is in the past, the verb shifts to the past perfect: *I wish I <u>had learned</u> to drive (but I didn't)*. Backshift operates with **modal verbs** in the same way: *I wish I <u>could</u> drive (but I can't). I wish it <u>would</u> rain (but it won't)*.

The verb *to wish*, followed by a *that*-clause, expresses an impossible or unlikely desire, so backshift is used. The verb *to hope*, on the other hand, expresses a desire that has the possibility of being fulfilled, so backshift is not necessary: *I hope it rains. She hopes you are well.*

Learners frequently confuse wishes and hopes, as in these examples from the Cambridge English Corpus:

> *I <u>wish</u> you agree with me. (= hope)*
> *Do you have a computer. I <u>wish</u> you have . So we can talk on the INTERNET. (= hope)*

Or they omit to use backshift when talking about unreal situations:

> *I wish I <u>haven't</u> said that. (= hadn't)*
> *My mother watch a lot TV these days ... I wish my mother <u>stop</u> watching. (= would stop)*

Backshift is also used in unreal **conditional clauses**, for the same purpose (see **43**): *If I <u>had</u> the time, I'd learn Korean (but I don't have the time). If I<u>'d known</u>, I would have phoned. (but I didn't know)*. Less obviously, it occurs in constructions such as *it's time*: *It's time you <u>had</u> a haircut.*

Should we avoid the passive?

George Orwell (1946) famously said 'Never use the passive where you can use the active'. But is it good advice?

The **passive** contrasts with the active and together they make up the system called **voice**. Voice is the way the 'actors' in a clause can be positioned. For example,

1 *Tolstoy wrote* War and Peace. = active
2 War and Peace *was written by Tolstoy.* = passive

The **subject** in (1) is Tolstoy; the subject in (2) is *War and Peace*. The passive turns the **verb's object** (*War and Peace*) into the subject. Yet the agent of the verb, i.e. the person performing the action, is Tolstoy in both cases.

There are many reasons for putting the object of the verb into the subject position. One reason might be because the agent is unknown, as in: *A car was set alight last night. The police were called.*

Another is that the agent is obvious or irrelevant:

> *The surgery was performed Sept. 7. The patient, whose name has not been revealed, was fully informed about the nature of the procedure.*

Or, the speaker or writer might not want to name the agent, perhaps in order to avoid incriminating them:

> *Tests showed his confession had been tampered with.*
> *He added: 'During the course of the party a lot of drink had been consumed.'*

Nevertheless, there are many contexts in which the active voice would sound awkward. For example, when describing certain processes:

> *When cocoa beans are ground, a sticky liquid is produced.*

Orwell, G. (1946). Politics and the English Language. *Horizon*, 13(76), 253–265

When do we use the long passive?

> Some grammars make the claim that the passive is used to move the focus of the clause on to the object of the verb: _Caesar was assassinated by Brutus_. Is this true?

Passive constructions make the **object** of the **verb** the grammatical **subject** (see **71**). The notional subject (or 'agent') is either not specified: _Caesar was assassinated,_ or is identified in a **prepositional phrase** after the verb: _Caesar was assassinated by Brutus_. The agent-less choice is known as the 'short passive'; the other as the 'long passive'.

Why should we choose to distribute the information using the long passive, rather than simply using the active: _Brutus assassinated Caesar_? After all, the informational content is exactly the same.

There are at least three reasons. The first is in order to maintain topic consistency. If a text is about Julius Caesar, it is likely that he will be the topic – and the grammatical subject – of most **clauses**. A text about Cleopatra, on the other hand, would likely feature fewer clauses with Caesar as subject.

The second reason is called the principle of **_end-focus_**. This means that, very generally, there is a tendency to place given information (i.e. information that is already familiar to the reader or listener) at the beginning of a clause and new information at the end. Compare the two versions of the same text below. The second version is more coherent because it places new information at the end, and uses the long passive to do this:

1 War and Peace _is a great novel. Leo Tolstoy wrote it._
2 War and Peace _is a great novel. It was written by Leo Tolstoy_.

The third reason is called **_end-weight_**: the longer and more complex a clause is, the more likely it is to go at the end: War and Peace _was written by the Russian nobleman, mystic and moralist Leo Tolstoy_ rather than _The Russian nobleman, mystic and moralist Leo Tolstoy wrote_ War and Peace.

What is the get-passive?

> Most passive constructions are formed with the auxiliary
> verb *be* plus the past participle. But there are other ways
> of forming the passive, including the use of *get.*

Here are some examples of the so-called *get*-**passive**, with some of the
verbs that are most frequently found in this construction:

> *Her friends are <u>getting married</u> and having babies, and she isn't.*
> *One player <u>got hit</u> in the ear by an egg.*
> *The advantage of the train is that it doesn't <u>get stuck</u> in traffic.*
> *I'm sorry I didn't <u>get involved</u> in the movement earlier.*

The *get*-passive is more frequent in informal contexts, particularly
conversation, and is often associated with negative experiences. Rather
than describing states (*Her friends <u>are</u> married …*), the *get*-passive
focuses on the process of arriving at that state. This extract of informal
talk is typical:

> *We ended up getting into a situation where, you know, we <u>got shoved</u>
> around, you know, <u>roughed up</u>. Ended up <u>getting taken</u> to the local
> precinct, had our parents called and everything, and you know, just a
> bad experience.*

The extract also includes another 'pseudo-passive' construction: *[they]
had our parents called* – what is sometimes called *the causative*: *have* or
get + **object** + *-ed*. This is often used when talking about services that
people have done for them, but also about events that happen to them:

> *We thought perhaps we ought to <u>have the kitchen redecorated</u>.*
> *She <u>gets her hair done</u> every week and <u>her nails done</u> every week.*
> *One day, Jen <u>had her camera stolen</u>, pick-pocketed.*

Another pseudo-passive construction is *need* + *-ing*, as in *The system
<u>needs fixing</u>*, which means the same as the passive construction *The
system needs to be fixed.*

F: Syntax

Grammar is traditionally considered to embrace two major linguistic systems: morphology, that is, the forms of words, including their inflections; and syntax: the way that these words combine into phrases, into clauses and into sentences, and the way that these combinations of elements function to make meaning. This section deals with questions that relate to syntax.

74   What are parts of speech?

> **Parts of speech is the old-fashioned name for word classes.**

The division of words into different types varies in some details, according to which theory of grammar is being applied, but there is general agreement as to the main categories. First of all, a distinction is made between closed classes and open classes. Closed classes are those that don't – or rarely – admit new members, and include what are called function words – such as **articles, prepositions,** and **pronouns.** The open class words, on the other hand, are continuously being renewed, and consist of lexical, or content, words, such as **nouns** and **verbs.**

Here, then, are the eight classes (for definitions see **Glossary**):

open classes	**nouns:** *car, Victoria, style, globalization ...*
	verbs: *think, collide, become, contain ...*
	adjectives: *blue, noisy, expensive, interesting ...*
	adverbs: *slowly, away, just, now ...*
closed classes	**pronouns:** *she, ours, anyone, who ...*
	determiners: *that, my, some, the, two ...*
	prepositions: *in, after, by, under ...*
	conjunctions: *and, while, if, because ...*

Some grammars also add interjections: *wow! ouch!*

It's important to note, though, that these categories are very fuzzy and there is a good deal of overlap between categories (see **29, 31,** and **40**).

Language description and language teaching tend to focus on sentences. But what exactly is a sentence?

Sentences – at least of the written kind – are easier to recognize than define. In spoken language, in particular, the concept of the 'well-formed sentence' is elusive – one reason why linguists prefer the term *utterance*.

Most sentences begin with a capital letter and end with a full stop – like this one. However, there are a number of other criteria, which these sentences written by learners fail to meet:

1   *There a lot of historical places in Antalya and Side.*
2   *You moving to a new shool. Yes or No?*
3   *I like animals is dogs.*
4   *Because there are a lot of touristic places and comfortable hotels.*
5   *But in Durham was very cold.*

Minimally, sentences need to have one main **verb**, which is not the case in (1). Also, the verb needs to be **finite**, i.e. one that is marked for **tense** and agrees with its **subject** in terms of number, which is not the case with (2). Two finite verbs in the same **clause** are not possible (3). A **subordinate clause** cannot stand alone as a sentence in its own right (4). And, except in the case of **imperatives**, the main verb must have a subject (5). In grammatical terms, then, a sentence must consist of a subject and its **predicate**, i.e. whatever is said about the subject.

Sentence structures are classified as simple, if they have one main clause: *Durham was very cold*. They are classified as compound, if they consist of two or more clauses joined by coordinating **conjunctions**, such as *and, but, or*. *It was very cold* and *it started to snow*. And they are complex, if they have a main clause and one or more subordinate (or dependent clauses): *When we were in Durham*, *it was very cold*.

Sentences can be either declarative (*Durham was cold*), interrogative (*What was Durham like?*), **imperative** (*Go to Durham!*) or exclamatory (*What a lovely town Durham is!*).

What is a clause?

> Because of the difficulties of defining a sentence,
> grammarians tend to prefer to analyse language at the level
> of the clause. This is not without its problems either!

A simple definition of a **clause** is any group of words that includes
a **verb**. Most clauses also contain a **subject** (S) as well. Other clause
elements, identified by their function, are **objects** (O), **complements** (C)
and **adverbials** (A) (see also **79** and **80**).

Sentences (see **75**) always consist of at least one clause. Two or more
clauses of equal rank can be linked (or coordinated) by a **conjunction**
like *and, or, but*. A **subordinate clause**, on the other hand, is dependent
on a main clause and can't stand alone as a sentence: *It happened <u>when
Harry met Sally</u>*.

There are four main kinds of subordinate clause:

- **adverbial clause**: *It happened <u>when Harry met Sally</u>*.
- **relative clause** (see **84**): *It happened to the man <u>who shot Liberty
  Valance</u>*.
- **complement clause** (also known as nominal clause): *I know <u>what
  you did last summer</u>*.
- comparative clauses: *It was stranger <u>than you think</u>*.

Depending on the verb, a clause can be finite or **non-finite**. A finite
clause contains a finite verb, i.e. one that is marked for **tense** and agrees
with its subject: *The postman always <u>rings</u> twice*.

A non-finite clause is one that has a **participle** or an **infinitive** as its verb:
*<u>Having rung once</u>, he rang again. <u>To be on the safe side</u>, he rang a third
time*.

Occasionally, the verb can be left out, to form a verbless clause: *<u>When
in doubt</u>, ring twice*.

> Dave Willis (2003) wrote: 'Learners need to sort out the patterns which follow verbs, and to assign verbs to those patterns'. What exactly are these patterns?

The choice of a **verb** commits the writer or speaker to a limited set of options. The verb *hit*, for example, requires an **object**: it's not enough to say **Kim hit*. The verb *go*, on the other hand, cannot take an object (it is **intransitive**) and, instead, is commonly followed by a **prepositional phrase**: *They went into town*. Some verbs require a whole **clause**: *I hope you pass your test*. For others there may be choice between two or more continuations, with some differences of meaning: *She remembered to call her mother* v *She remembered calling her mother*.

These different combinations are called verb patterns.

Some of the more common patterns, and the verbs that typically take them, are listed below. (V = verb; C = **complement**; O = object; A = **adverbial**; NP = **noun phrase**)

Pattern	Typical verbs	Example
V	*happen, wake up*	*What happened?*
V + C	*be, seem, look*	*You seem tired.*
V + O (NP)	*do, have, eat, hit*	*Have a shower.*
V + O (-*ing*)	*like, enjoy, remember*	*He likes rowing.*
V + O (*to-* infinitive)	*want, agree, hope*	*I hope to win.*
V + O (*that*-clause)	*say, suggest, think*	*They say (that) it will rain.*
V + O + O	*give, tell, teach, send*	*Send me an email.*
V + O + A	*put, throw, push*	*Don't throw it away.*
V + A	*go, stay, fall*	*She stayed three weeks.*
V + O + C	*elect, name, call*	*They named her Eve.*

Willis, D. (2003). *Rules, Patterns and Words*. Cambridge: Cambridge University Press.

> Words seldom occur in isolation: they tend to hunt in
> packs. And these packs are called phrases. So, what is a
> phrase, and how many types are there?

The following extract from John Buchan's novel *The Thirty-Nine Steps*
consists of a sequence of words, which can be segmented into **clauses,**
each with its own **verb** (see **76**):

> [As we <u>moved</u> away from that station [my companion <u>woke</u> up.]]
> [He <u>fixed</u> me with a wandering glance], [<u>kicked</u> his dog viciously,]
> and [<u>inquired</u> [where he <u>was</u>.]] [Clearly he <u>was</u> very drunk.]

The individual words that comprise the clauses bunch together into
phrases consisting of a **head** word and the words that go before and
after it. So, (ignoring the conjunctions that connect the clauses), a
phrase-level analysis produces:

> / we / moved away / from that station / my companion / woke up / …
> / Clearly / he / was / very drunk /

All five types of phrase are represented here, each identified by the word
class that comprises its head:

> **Noun phrases** (NPs): <u>we</u>, that <u>station</u>, my <u>companion</u>, <u>he</u>
> **Verb phrases** (VPs): <u>moved</u> away, <u>woke</u> up, <u>was</u>
> **Prepositional phrase** (PP): <u>from</u> that station
> **Adverb phrase:** (AdvP): <u>clearly</u>
> **Adjective** phrase: (AdjP): very <u>drunk</u>

Some phrases consist of single words, e.g. *clearly.* But they could be
extended by means of modification: *very clearly.* Also some phrases are
embedded in others: *from [that station]*, where *that station* is a NP.

A phrase analysis allows us to see how sentences are organized into
units of meaning, which in turn allows us to assign functions to these
units such as **subject, object, complement** or **adverbial.**

What is a complement?

> The term *complement* comes from the verb *to complete*.
> What exactly is being completed and with what?

The term *complement* has a range of meanings, depending which kind of grammar you consult. In most grammars, the complement is one of the five elements of **clause** structure (see **76**). Typically it is the clause element that follows linking **verbs**, such as *be* and *seem*: it 'complements' (i.e. completes) the verb by providing further information about the **subject**: *Caesar was <u>a Roman</u>.* ('*Caesar was*' on its own doesn't make much sense.) Compare this with *Caesar married a Roman*, where *a Roman* is the **object** of the verb. Or *Caesar went to Rome*, where *to Rome* is an **adverbial**.

Complements are typically **noun** phrases: *Rome is <u>the capital of Italy</u>*; and **adjective** phrases: *Caesar proved to be <u>ruthless</u>*; but they can also be clauses: *What Caesar did was <u>conquer Gaul</u>.*

A further distinction is made between complements of the subject (as in the above examples, where the complement adds more information about the subject) and complements of the object, where the complement adds more information about the object: *The Senate appointed him <u>dictator</u>. Caesar named Octavian <u>his heir</u>.*

In some contemporary grammars, a complement is any obligatory element required to complete the **head** of a **phrase**. This is seen in **prepositional phrases**, where a noun phrase functions as the complement of a **preposition** (*across <u>the Rubicon</u>; into <u>the Senate</u>*).

In verb phrases it is seen in the way, for example, **transitive** verbs take obligatory direct object complements: *Caesar conquered <u>Gaul</u>.* With other verbs, the complement might be a *to*-**infinitive**: *Caesar was planning <u>to invade Parthia</u>.* Or it might be what is called a ***complement clause***, typically a *that*-clause: *Caesar was warned <u>that he would be assassinated</u>.* These complementation patterns are discussed in **77**.

80 | What is the difference between an adverb and an adverbial?

And, for that matter, what is difference between an adverb phrase and an adverbial?

Adverbs are members of a word class (see **74**) which typically describe the circumstances of an action, answering questions like *When? Where? How?* e.g. *Suddenly he frowned. He ushered me indoors. I watched them carefully.* Or they precede a word or phrase to express degree: *He looked really shocked; I was rather a success.* (Examples are from John Buchan's *The Thirty-Nine Steps*.)

When an adverb forms the **head** of a **phrase** (see **78**), the combination is called an **adverb phrase**: *I wanted it pretty badly; You might have looked more closely; It was taking me too far north.*

An **adverbial**, on the other hand, is one of the five possible elements in a **clause** (see **76**). Like an adverb, an adverbial (1) contributes circumstantial information to the clause, such as time, place or manner: *Then with some difficulty I turned the car;* or (2) it serves to comment on what is being expressed: *Happily there were few people about;* or (3) it links clauses to some other component of the text: *I did not give him very close attention. The fact is, I was more interested in … .*

The most common way of forming adverbials are:

1 adverbs and adverb phrases: *Frankly, Hannay, I don't believe that part of his story.*
  Now and then a sheep wandered off;
2 **prepositional phrases**: *My guest was lying sprawled on his back. There was a long knife through his heart;*
3 some **noun phrases**: *Next day he was much more cheerful;*
4 **clauses**: *When he came back we dined together.*

So: adverbs are individual words; an adverb phrase is a group of words whose head is an adverb; and an adverbial is any word, phrase or clause that functions like an adverb.

Where do adverbials go?

Adverbials are highly flexible, but there are constraints on where they can go.

There are three positions that **adverbs** and **adverb phrases** can take:

- initial: before the **subject**: _Suddenly he looked at his watch_;
- mid: either between the subject and the **verb**: _He suddenly sprang to his feet_, or between the **auxiliary** and the main verb: _The dog had suddenly turned_; or after the verb _to be_: _His manner was suddenly genial_.
- final: after the verb and any **object** or **complement**: _Holmes turned suddenly to the right_.

(Examples are from Conan Doyle's _The Return of Sherlock Holmes_.)

Note that it is not usual to put an adverb between a verb and its object or other obligatory elements:

> *I packed _quickly_ some of my belongings.
> *In his young age he went _often_ to France.

There are restrictions on which adverbs can go in which position. The most common position is final. Adverbs that prefer the mid position are those concerned with likelihood: _The man was probably in London._ Linking adverbs tend to take initial position: _Finally he drove round to the Charing Cross telegraph office._

When two or more adverbials occupy the final position, the usual order is: manner (i.e. how?), place (where?) and time (when?):

> _The wind whistled shrilly down the long street._
> _Meet us at Baker Street at six o'clock this evening._
> _Holmes and I sat together in silence all the evening._

I gave *her* a book: what is the direct object?

> Verbs in English are intransitive, monotransitive or ditransitive: they take no object, one object, or two objects.

A ditransitive **verb** takes two **objects**: *Ford paid his workers decent wages.* Here the direct object (*decent wages*) follows the indirect object (*his workers*). Indirect objects generally denote the people who receive or benefit from the action of the verb.

Ditransitive verbs can take an alternative structure, in which the indirect object becomes the **complement** of a **prepositional phrase**, starting with *to* or *for*: *Ontarians pay taxes <u>to the federal government</u>.*

Here are some examples of ditransitive verbs alongside the equivalent prepositional phrase structures, with the indirect objects underlined:

Ditransitive verbs	Prepositional phrases
Zola then gave <u>the home</u> side the lead.	*So I gave the ball <u>to him</u> and let him do the rest.*
Lincoln sent <u>his wife</u> a check.	*He has sent his videos <u>to CNN</u>.*
Can you read <u>me</u> the first paragraph?	*Wanda read passages <u>to me</u> when I was there.*
You don't owe <u>me</u> a penny.	*I felt I owed a lot <u>to the Navy</u>.*
Someone bought <u>her</u> a bus ticket.	*I buy a lot of clothes <u>for her</u>.*

The choice of which construction to use may depend on emphasis: the principle of **end-focus**, whereby new or important information goes to the end of the sentence, may favour the use of the prepositional phrase: *He altered his will to leave his entire fortune <u>to his new wife</u>.* Likewise, the principle of **end-weight** favours putting a long indirect object after, rather than before, a short direct object: *Your father has decided to read us <u>the chapter in Proverbs in praise of a virtuous wife</u>.*

Where there are two **pronouns**, the tendency is to put the direct object first: *Well, don't show <u>it</u> to them. You can send <u>it</u> to me later.*

When can we leave out relative pronouns?

> Relative pronouns are those pronouns that attach a relative clause to the head noun in a noun phrase, as in *the house that Jack built*. Omission of the pronoun is possible under certain circumstances.

There are five relative **pronouns** in English: *which, who, whom, whose, that*. In addition, there are three relative **adverbs**: *where, when*, and *why*. As well as connecting the **relative clause** to its preceding **noun**, they play a grammatical role in the **clause** itself, as **subject** or **object**, for example.

The relative pronoun can be omitted in cases where it stands for the object, or indirect object, or prepositional object. In these examples, 'zero relatives' are marked Ø:

	Grammatical role	Omission
He had a girlfriend Ø he wanted to marry.	object	*who/whom*
The last guy Ø I gave my number to at a party called the next day.	indirect object	*who*
They were sharing a room in the apartment Ø they were living in.	object of a preposition	*which*

If the relative clause is a non-defining one (see **84**), then pronoun omission is not possible:

> *He was with his girlfriend, <u>whom</u> I rather liked.*
> *Now I am living in a $175,000 apartment, <u>which</u> I own.*

Relative pronoun omission is common in spoken language, especially where the relative clause begins with a personal pronoun (as in the examples above).

What is a non-defining relative clause?

And how does it differ from a defining relative clause, in speech and in writing?

When it is important to identify the referent of a **noun phrase,** this can be done using either pre- or post-modification or both: *Our office is rife with gossip about my best friend at work.* (see **11**).

One common way of identifying the referent is to post-modify the **noun** with a **relative clause** (also called an **adjective** clause): *Are you the friend who lives in Canada?*

Because the relative clause identifies or defines the referent, it is called *a defining* (or *restrictive*) *relative clause.* Not all relative clauses have this defining function:

He was encouraged by a friend, who had heard him sing, to take lessons.

This is a non-defining relative clause: it simply adds extra information – indicated by the use of commas in writing, or by intonation, when spoken. The clause can usually be omitted without significant loss of meaning: *He was encouraged by a friend to take lessons.*

Non-defining relative clauses have other characteristics that distinguish them from defining relative clauses:

- the **object** relative **pronoun** cannot be omitted (see **83**):

  She has one friend Ø she loves to play with. = defining
  His best friend, whom he loved not unlike a lover, died. = non-defining

- the relative pronoun cannot be *that*:

  He is being counselled by a friend, who is a nun. = non-defining (not **that is a nun*)

A special kind of non-defining relative clause, called a *sentence relative,* refers, not to a preceding noun, but to a whole clause: *The judge was very lenient, which I thought was real fair.*

Tell a non-specialist that you are writing a book about grammar and their first question is: 'Is it about the difference between *who* and *whom*?'

Even as far back as 1891, when he wrote his *New English Grammar* Henry Sweet acknowledged the disappearance of *whom* as an interrogative **pronoun**: '*Who* has an objective case *whom*, parallel to *him*, for which, however, the uninflected *who* is substituted in the spoken language, as in *who(m) do you mean?*'.

Over a century later, *whom* is proving surprisingly resilient, even in spoken language – not so much as an interrogative pronoun (*Whom do you mean?*) but as a relative pronoun (see **83**), as in these examples:

1 *She employs fifteen staff, most of whom are part-time.*
2 *They were Jews of whom very little is known.*
3 *I'm one of the lucky ones for whom medication works.*

As in all these examples, *whom* is frequently used as the **object** of a **preposition**, and particularly in quantitative constructions: *both of whom, some of whom, one of whom,* etc. *Which* is a possible alternative for example (1), but not for (2) and (3), which – to avoid the use of *whom* – would need to be reformulated.

Nevertheless, *whom* is often used unnecessarily, resulting in usage that sounds pretentious, such as the following:

I just kind of have to reach inside and make sure that I hold on to whom I am as a person.
I think there are people for whom I have a great respect for.
All families, regardless of whom they may be, suffer different kinds of problems.

Sweet, H. (1891, 1968) *New English Grammar: Part 1: Introduction, Phonology and Accidence.* Oxford: Clarendon Press.

What's wrong with *I don't know where is the bank?*

> Question forms are difficult for learners, given inversion and the use of auxiliary verbs. It must be frustrating to discover that these rules no longer apply in indirect questions.

One of the single most persistent errors learners make is overgeneralizing question forms in indirect, or reported questions, as in these examples:

1 *I didn't know <u>where was car parking lot</u>.*
2 *Do you know <u>where is my uncle's shop</u>?*
3 *Can you tell me <u>how much is the ticket</u>?*
4 *You asked me <u>what time should you</u> come.*
5 *I ran back and asked him <u>where did he find</u> the diary.*

First, let's review the rules of question formation in main **clauses**. If the main **verb** is a form of *to be*, invert the **subject** and verb: *How much <u>is the ticket</u>?* If the main verb has an **auxiliary**, invert the auxiliary and subject: *What time <u>should I</u> come?* If there is no auxiliary, insert a form of *do*, and invert this with the subject: *Where <u>did you</u> find the diary?*

In **subordinate clauses**, such as those that report speech (or thought), or in indirect (or embedded) questions, the rules of inversion no longer apply: the word order of affirmative sentences, where the subject precedes the verb, is maintained:

> *I didn't know where <u>the parking lot was</u>.*
> *You asked me what time <u>you should</u> come.*
> *I asked him where <u>he found</u> [or <u>he had</u> found] the diary.*

In fact, in spoken language, these 'rules' are occasionally broken, as speakers blend direct and indirect speech:

> *This woman asked me <u>where's a bank machine for my bank</u>.*
> *I would like to know <u>where is all this data going to be stored</u>?*
> *Can you tell me <u>who is she</u>.*

When do we use *backshift* in reported speech?

> *Backshift* is the process whereby the present becomes the past, and the past becomes the past perfect.

When speech is reported, it is often from the perspective of another person, place, and time. This might involve changes like the use of **tense** backshift, as well as other features that 'distance' the context:

> *An officer told her he could not find the previous day's missing person report and she had to file another one.*

The direct speech version of the officer's words may have been: '*I can't find yesterday's missing person report. You have to file another one*'.

Typical features of reported speech include:

- **quotatives**: *An officer <u>told</u> her … he <u>said</u> … I'<u>m like</u> …*
- tense backshift: *can → could; have → had*
- third person **pronouns**: *I → he; you → she*
- time **adverbials**: *yesterday → the previous day*
- demonstratives and place adverbials: e.g. *this → that; here → there*
- no inversion in questions (see **86**): *Where do you live? → I asked where she lived.*

However, depending on the reporting person's assessment of the degree of distance, in terms of time, place, person and current relevance, these operations might not be applicable:

> *She told me she's staying with her mum.* (not *was staying*)
> *You just said somebody told you this.*
> *Peter said he'll take me.*
> *I asked her if she's ready to support Barack Obama.*

In spoken language, indirect speech is relatively uncommon: speakers prefer to reproduce the speaker's exact words, or sense of them:

> *She said, she looked at it and she says <u>you're not having that</u>. I said <u>I am</u>. I said <u>when are you coming round to see us</u>? And he goes, <u>oh</u>, he goes <u>well whenever</u>.*

88 When can we omit *that*?

And what is a *that*-clause?

That-clauses are a kind of **complement clause** (also called *noun clause* or *nominal clause*) that 'completes' the meaning of **verbs** like *think, agree,* and *say,* as well as of some **nouns** (*argument, claim*) and **adjectives** (*sure, certain*). The **conjunction** *that* is often omitted. Compare:

1a *I know that you don't like my terminology.*
1b *I know you don't like the movie.*

2a *He was pretty sure that Michel was gay.*
2b *Are you sure you want to go?*

Sentences (1b) and (2b) display '*that*-omission', i.e. the omission of the conjunction *that.* (Note that this is not the same use of *that* as in **relative clauses**: *the keys that I lost*: see **83**.)

That-omission is most common in spoken language and relatively uncommon in academic writing. In speech, it is most likely to occur after the verbs *say* and *think,* and/or when the subjects of each clause are the same, and/or take the form of personal **pronouns**, as in these examples (where *that*-omission is represented by Ø):

> *She said Ø she liked the show.*
> *I think Ø I'll stick around.*

Retention of *that,* on the other hand, is more likely – even in spoken language – if there is more than one *that*-clause in the sequence:

> *I doubt Ø this policy will work, or <u>that</u> it would be desirable if it did.*

Retention is also more likely in **passive** constructions:

> *She was warned <u>that</u> she would be charged with trespassing.*

That may be omitted after adjectives but rarely after nouns:

> *We were not aware Ø there was a problem.*

> *The fact <u>that</u> you said that is so bizarre.*

What is inversion and when is it used?

> *Inversion* is a syntactic process where two components of a clause switch places. It has a number of purposes.

The most common form of inversion in English is **subject-verb** inversion in the formation of questions: *Are you hungry?* This once involved inverting the main verb with the subject. Since the sixteenth century, however, the operation has been limited to the **auxiliary verb** only, or, in the absence of an auxiliary verb, the 'dummy' auxiliary *do* (see **41**).

Learners find the system of 'subject and auxiliary only inversion' difficult to master:

> *And when <u>you will</u> arrive? (= will you)*
> *So how <u>your new job is</u> going? (= is your new job)*
> *Where <u>you have</u> been ? (= have you)*

The system is complicated by the fact that, in indirect questions, there is no inversion: *Can you tell me where there's a church?* (see **86**).

Other uses of inversion in English are much less common and are mostly limited to more formal or literary registers. They include **subject-auxiliary** inversion in unreal **conditionals**, and after initial **adverbials** with a negative or 'near-negative' sense:

> <u>Had I</u> *known that, I wouldn't have done it.*
> *Never <u>had I</u> experienced such blind terror.*
> *Very seldom <u>do you</u> see a female wearing a hat anymore.*

Inversion of the subject and the main verb is used when an adverbial of place is 'fronted' in order to put new information after the verb – according to the principle of **end-focus**:

> *In the third row <u>sat a tall, slight, unimposing man</u>.*
> *Here <u>comes the bus</u>.*

What is a question tag?

In informal spoken interaction, speakers frequently seek confirmation and agreement, and monitor understanding and interest, through the use of question tags. Don't they?

Questions tags are formed from an **auxiliary verb** (see **37**) plus a **subject pronoun**, which repeats the subject of the main **clause**. If the verb in the main clause is affirmative, the tag is usually negative, and vice versa:

> *Oh sometimes I like a fresh sort of breeze. I mean, it's nice, <u>isn't it</u>?*
> *Well he won't do anything, <u>will he</u>?*
> *I forgot about it though, really. You do though, <u>don't you</u>?*
> *You can't say fairer than that, <u>can you</u>?*

As well as having an interpersonal function, question tags are also used, like genuine questions, to check or clarify information:

> *You don't smoke a lot though, <u>do you</u>?*
> *Aristotle talked about them, <u>didn't he</u>?*
> *He was a bishop, <u>wasn't he</u>?*

Or to make requests: *You couldn't stay a little bit longer Helen, <u>could you</u>?*

When the speaker is checking an inference, the tag can take the same polarity (e.g. affirmative) as the main clause: *They're happy with you, <u>are they</u>?*

The intonation of interpersonal tags, i.e. those that are designed to elicit agreement, is usually a fall; in real questions and requests it is a rise:

> *Oh gosh I'm harping on, aren't I ?* ↘
> *I'm the first, aren't I?* ↗

Why is it *What happened?*, not *What did happen?*

> Having learned that questions are formed by the inversion of the subject and the auxiliary, learners then discover that some questions don't, in fact, invert. Why?

Wh-questions are so-called because they typically begin with a question word like *what, when, where* – as well as *how*. The question words target different elements of a sentence or **clause**. For example, to elicit information contained in this sentence: *In 1928 Alexander Fleming discovered penicillin in his laboratory by chance,* we can ask about the **object**: *What did he discover?*, about the **adverbial** elements: *Where/ When/How did he discover penicillin?* and also about the **subject**: *Who discovered penicillin?*

Because subject questions target the first element in the clause – the subject – no inversion of the subject and **auxiliary verb** is required, as in other kinds of questions:

> Object question: *Fleming discovered something* → *Fleming discovered what?* → *What did Fleming discover?*

> Subject question: *Somebody discovered penicillin* → *Who discovered penicillin?*

Other examples of subject questions include: *What happened to your arm? Who's coming for a swim? Which costs less? Who called?*

Of course, the question *What did happen?* is acceptable in contexts where extra emphasis is required: *No one certainly had any idea what was going to happen next. ~ And what did happen next?*

Nor is lack of inversion exclusive to subject questions: statement (or declarative) *yes/no* questions also follow standard 'subject first' word order, typically with a rising intonation:

> *So you're not from LA originally?*
> *You don't like it here?*

92 What does *there* mean in *there's no one here?*

There seems to be a contradiction here: how can something be here and there at the same time?

There are two distinct meanings and uses of *there*. Like *here*, *there* is an **adverb** that indicates a place – in the case of *there*, a place at a distance from the immediate context: *I live there with my grandmother.* (All the examples are from John Buchan's *The Thirty-Nine Steps*.)

And then there is its use to state the existence of something – called *existential there*: *There were two policemen at the door. There might be trouble.* Sometimes both meanings can coexist in the same sentence: *There was nobody there or any sign of an owner.*

The existential use of *there* is a way of placing the **subject** after the **verb,** in line with the principle of **end-focus,** so that the information flow moves from 'given' to 'new'. It would be grammatically correct to say *Two policeman were at the door.* But this would give *at the door* more prominence than the two policemen. So *there* acts as a **dummy subject** (see **93**): *There were two policeman at the door.* The fact that it is the grammatical subject is shown in the way it is inverted to make questions: *Were there two policeman at the door?*

Existential *there* should not be confused with the use of 'fronted' place **adverbials** (see **89**), as in *There stood the car, very spick and span.*

Existential *there* is typically used to introduce new information, in the form of an indefinite **noun phrase**, often accompanied by an adverbial of place: *There was a man on the platform whose looks I didn't like.* It is also used to introduce items in a series:

> *With the torch to help me I investigated further. There were bottles and cases of queer-smelling stuffs, [...] and there were coils of fine copper wire.[...] There was a box of detonators, and a lot of cord for fuses.*

Sometimes, and especially in fiction, verbs other than *be* are used: *I hadn't waited long till there came another ring at the bell.*

In *it's raining*, what does the *it* stand for?

> *It's raining* enshrines two basic principles of English syntax: end-focus and non-pro-drop.

It could be argued that *it* stands for the weather, or even the rain, but in fact, it stands for nothing: it's simply a placeholder to allow the important or new information to come after the **verb**. That's the principle of **end-focus**, i.e. that the default setting for distributing information in a sentence is from 'given' to 'new' (see also **92**). As in this short exchange:

I've bought a new car.   ~ Oh? What make?   ~ It's a Volvo.

It, referring to the new car, is now a given by virtue of having been mentioned already. The new information comes after the verb: *a Volvo*. Reversing the order sounds like nonsense: **A Volvo is it.*

The same is the case for *it's raining*, where 'raining' is the new information so it comes at the end. The problem is that there is no given information to refer to to put at the beginning. Moreover, English is a 'non-pro-drop' language, which means that **pronouns** cannot be dropped from the **subject** slot, a 'dummy pronoun' has to be enlisted to fill the otherwise vacant slot: *It's raining*.

Dummy *it* (also called *nonreferential it*) features in a number of constructions used to talk about time, distance and the environment:

It's nine o'clock.
It takes two hours to get there.

It's also used in some constructions where an entire **clause** that is the **subject** of the sentence is moved to the end of the sentence: *It's strange you haven't heard of him.* Which, put another way, means *That you haven't heard of him is strange.*

94   What is a cleft sentence?

> There are a number of different ways of drawing attention
> to the important content in a sentence. Clefting is one.

Clefts are sentences or **clauses** that have been split in two to make two clauses (hence, *cleft*, from the **verb** *to cleave*), so as to redistribute their content, often for the purposes of making a contrast. For example:

> *It's great that I've found a strong woman, but <u>what I really need is a strong man</u>.*

Because new or important information usually goes at the end of the clause, clefting allows two focal points, not just one: *what I <u>really need</u> is <u>a strong man</u>*. Compare this to ... *but I really need a strong man.*

There are two kinds of clefts:

- *wh*-clefts (sometimes called pseudo-clefts): – as in the above example;
- *it*-clefts: *I know he would've waited, but <u>it was me who didn't want to wait</u>.*

In this case, the focus is on the **complement** of *was*: *me* (not *he*). Compare the less forceful: ... *but I didn't want to wait.*

Wh-clefts are common in spoken language:

> *What you should do is take it back to the shop.*
> *What we really need are more community colleges.*

It-clefts, on the other hand, are most common in academic writing:

> *It is Plato who argues about the perpetual yearning of the soul.*

G: Miscellaneous

Finally, in this section are a few questions that aren't easily categorized, partly because at least some of them hover in the grey area between vocabulary and grammar, or between grammar and discourse.

---

95 When do we use *take* and when *bring*?

96 Why *at 5 o'clock*, but *on Monday* and *in January*?

97 What is the difference between *for* and *since*?

98 Are *but* and *however* the same?

99 What's the difference between *if* and *unless*?

100 What does *up* mean in *drink it up*?

101 What part of speech is *like*?

When do we use *take* and when *bring*?

Or *come* and *go*, or *this* and *that*, or *here* and *there*, i.e.
words whose use must take into account the relative
position of the addressor and addressee?

When we speak, we 'point' with language, indicating, for example,
whether we perceive something as near us (*this one here*) or distant
(*that one there*). The focal point of orientation is where the speaker (or
writer) is. Some **verbs** of motion, such as *bring/take*, and *come/go*, also
imply direction either to or away from the speaker: *Bring it closer! Take
it away! Come to bed! Go to bed!*

It is not the case, however, that *come* and *bring* refer simply to
movement towards the speaker (to *here*), while *go* and *take* refer to
movement away from the speaker (to *there*). With these particular **verbs**
the point of orientation is both where I am and where you are, so that
we say both *Come over here* [i.e. to my place] *and bring pizza* and *I'll
come over there* [i.e. to your place] *and bring pizza*. However, in the
case of a third place, where neither of us are, we would normally say
Go over there and take them pizza.

In many languages, such as Spanish, there is only one point of
orientation, and movement away from it is always 'going'. So, in
Spanish, *I'm coming* (*to you*) would be translated by the equivalent of
the verb *to go*: *voy* (literally *I go*).

Unsurprisingly, learners have problems negotiating this system, as these
errors from the Cambridge English Corpus show:

> *I know an interesting place near my house. If you came here, I'll <u>bring</u>
> you to there!* (= *take*)

> *It happened ten years ago during my last stay in Warsaw. I <u>came</u> there
> to visit my brother Peter...* (= *went*)

> *I have just arrived here on my holiday. I <u>went</u> here by plane.* (= *came*)

> *Sam, You have to come to my house at night. It is better you <u>take</u>
> sweaters because here is cold.* (= *bring*)

Why *at 5 o'clock*, but *on Monday* and *in January*?

> Prepositions cause more grief to learners than perhaps any other area of language. The choice of preposition often seems quite random. But is it?

Prepositions were originally designed to talk about relations in space, of which there are three dimensions: 1. points, 2. lines and surfaces, and 3. volumes (including enclosed areas). The prototypical 'point preposition' is *at*: *at the station. On* is the most common 'line and surface preposition': *on Main Street, on the table.* And *in* relates to enclosed spaces: *in the cupboard.*

Unlike space, time is invisible and intangible: in order to talk about it, therefore, we think about it metaphorically as a kind of space, having points, lines and surfaces, and area or volume. As such, we borrow space prepositions to talk about time:

- as points: *at 4 o'clock, at noon, at/by/around midnight*;
- as a surface: *on Sunday; on our holiday*;
- as a container: *in 2001, in the afternoon, in September, in midwinter.*

We can also move to and from points of time (*from one second to the next*), or out of a container of time: *out of the past*. Like place, we can also conceptualize the same time in different ways, so that it would be possible to say both *to the future* and *into the future*, or (as in some varieties of English) *in the weekend*, or *on the weekend*, rather than *at the weekend*.

As an example of the varied ways of conceptualizing time, here are some examples:

> *The statewide forecast calls for a chance of light rain or snow Saturday night and <u>into Sunday</u>.* (= volume)
> *Will that be ready by the end of the morning or are we looking <u>at Tuesday morning</u> for that?* (= point)
> *A man washes a car <u>on a rainy afternoon</u> in Sydney.* (= surface)
> *Does it matter if pupils go away <u>in term time</u>?* (= volume)
> *Maggie looked at her watch. It was just <u>on midnight</u>.* (= line or surface)

What is the difference between *for* and *since*?

This is another question about time prepositions – which also involves questions of tense choice.

Learners commonly confuse *for* and *since, from* and *ago*:

> *I do appologies that I have not seen you <u>since</u> a long time. (= for)*
> *It was <u>since six years</u> we had the opportunity to celebrate an occasion together. (= six years ago)*
> *She was my best friend 10 years ago. <u>For</u> that time I haven't got any message from her. (= Since)*
> *<u>For</u> the very first moment I found something really special about her. (= From)*

Both *for* and *since* are used to talk about duration, and answer the question *How long …?* Only *for* is used with the period of time: *for <u>three weeks</u>, for <u>ten minutes</u>, for <u>ages</u>,* etc. *Since,* on the other hand, is used with the point at which the period began: *since <u>last Tuesday</u>, since <u>3 o'clock</u>, since <u>they met</u>.*

Both *for* and *since* are commonly used with the present perfect to talk about periods that started in the past and continue to the present:

> *The band's been together <u>since 1994</u>.*
> *The band's been together <u>for 27 years</u>.*

However, unlike *since, for* can also be used to talk about periods of time in the past, present or future: *I'll be there <u>for three weeks</u>.* To talk about the starting point of periods other than those leading up to the present, *from* can be used: *From that time on I was hooked.*

Ago (an **adverb**) refers to a point in the past, and answers the question *When?* So *ago* is used with the past: *The band was formed <u>27 years ago</u>.*

But expressions with *ago* can mark the starting point of a period of time leading up to the present: *Membership has doubled since <u>we opened two years ago</u>.*

Are *but* and *however* the same?

> *But* and *however* serve as linking devices with a contrastive function. But they behave somewhat differently.

When speakers or writers link elements of a **phrase, clause,** or sentence, it can be for different purposes, such as addition (as in *They came and stayed*), reason and cause (*They stayed because they liked it*) and contrast (*They liked it but we didn't*). *But* and *however* share a contrastive function.

There are three main kinds of linking devices:

- coordinating **conjunctions,** such as *and, but, or,* that join equivalent parts of a sentence, such as two clauses: *It rained, but we had fun.*
- subordinating conjunctions, like *if, although, when,* that join a **subordinate clause** to a main clause: *If it rains, we'll eat inside.*
- linking **adverbs,** like *therefore* and *also,* that connect sentences: *It was late. It was also raining.*

This is where the difference lies: *but* is a conjunction whereas *however* is a linking adverb. *But* more often links clauses than sentences, whereas *however* links sentences only, and can take initial, mid or final position:

1 *It took some doing to get you safe here. However, that is all over now.*
2 *I found out nothing, however, about Henriques.*
3 *The fellow at my side was good-humoured enough ... I didn't want to talk, however.*

In (1) *But* could substitute for *However,* but not in (2) or (3).

However is also limited to formal or academic registers, whereas *but* is stylistically neutral. Learners tend to overuse *however* at the expense of *but* or *although*:

> *My house actually is OK , it's small however the right size for me because I'm alone.* (= *but*)
> *We went to a famous restaurant in Paris . It was expensive however really nice and tasty.* (= *but*)

99 What's the difference between *if* and *unless*?

> *Unless* is often presented as another way of saying *if ... not*. But this rather simplifies the issue.

The rule of thumb that *unless* means *if not* works some of the time, but it is only a part of the story and may account for these learner errors:

> *Your parents would be really disappointed <u>unless you go with them</u>.* (= *if you don't go with them*)
> *I suggest getting to work or school by bicycle if the journey doesn't take too long and <u>unless it rains</u>.* (= *if it doesn't rain*)

Rather than equating *unless* with *if not*, it is better to think of it as meaning *except if ...* or *except under these circumstances ...* So:

1 *I'll be at your place at 9.00, unless (= except if) the bus is late.*
2 *The front room was never used, unless (= except if) we had important visitors.*

In sentence (1) there is only one reason why I might not be at your place at 9.00, and that would be the bus being late. Likewise, in sentence (2) there was only one circumstance when the front room was used: when we had important visitors. But *unless* is unlikely here:

3 *I'll be angry if the bus isn't on time.*

In sentence (3) the bus not being on time is the *reason* for my being angry. On the other hand, the sentence:

4 *I'll be angry unless (= except if) the bus is on time.*

means: the only thing that will prevent me from being angry is the bus being on time – which sounds strange to say the least. Likewise, in

5 *Your parents would be really disappointed unless you go with them.*

means: the only thing that will prevent your parents from being disappointed is your going with them.

What does *up* mean in *drink it up?*

Or, more generally, do the particles in phrasal verbs –
back, out, over, in, on, etc. – have a meaning that is
independent of the main verb?

There's a joke about the woodsman who says, 'I cut trees down and
then I cut them up'. In what sense does he mean *up?* And does the *up* in
cut them up have anything to do with the *up* in *eat them up?*

There is a school of thought that argues that language is fashioned out
of our lived experience of the physical world, which is then generalized
to more abstract areas of experience – such as the way **prepositions** of
place are enlisted to express time relations (see **96**).

Verticality – represented by the word *up* – is one such mental model.
From an early age, we *look up, stand up,* and *jump up.* Verticality is
also associated with an increase in size and, by further extension, with
an increase in scale: you *grow up*; you *blow up* a balloon; the car *speeds
up,* the market is *picking up.* Increase in scale also occurs as things
approach us – they get bigger: people *walk up* to us. The combined
meanings of increase in scale and approach explain why *up* conveys a
sense of completeness: *drink up* your milk; *cut up* the logs.

Other **phrasal verb particles** (see **42**) express ideas that come from
physical experience. For example:

back: → what is behind me: *look back* → reverse movement: *stand
back, push back* → return movement: *come back, give back* → return
or reversal generally: *pay back, set back, date back*

out: → not in: *keep out, put (the cat) out, go out (for a meal)* →
emerging: *break out, come out* → spreading: *hand out, give out.* Also,
from 'not in' → disappearing: *put out (a fire), cross out, (the lights)
go out.*

101 What part of speech is *like*?

> *Like* is one of the most frequent and versatile words in the English language – partly because it has so many meanings and ranges over several different word classes.

Here are some examples from the Cambridge English Corpus of *like* in context:

1 *I don't <u>like</u> the way they yell at you and make you do push-ups.*
2 *I'd <u>like</u> a reservation for two for dinner.*
3 *She filled in a questionnaire about her <u>likes</u> and dislikes before going in front of the selection committee.*
4 *I recognize her face. She looks <u>like</u> her sister.*
5 *If you didn't do it <u>like</u> he wanted – your hands were cut off!*
6 *She's <u>like</u> 'Can I have some that are still frozen?' and I'm <u>like</u> 'Er yes but why on earth?'*
7 *I mean she's got <u>like</u> dementia and hasn't got a clue.*
8 *And that stuff is deadly <u>like</u>. And it ... we've got special skips there <u>like</u>.*

Like in (1) and (2) are recognizably **verbs**, with *I'd like* as a more polite way of saying *I want*. In (3) *like* is the **noun** derived from the same root: it has now acquired a secondary meaning as in *The video I uploaded got over a hundred <u>likes</u>.*

In (4) *like* functions as a **preposition**, meaning 'similar to': it's always followed by a **noun** or **pronoun**, although, unusually for a preposition, it can be modified by **adverbs** like *quite* or *rather*. *Like* in (5) is related, but acts as a subordinating **conjunction**: it is a less formal equivalent of *as* (and, as such, is frowned on by purists).

Examples (6), (7) and (8) are relatively recent usages and are more often spoken than written: in (6) *like* is an informal **quotative**, i.e. a word that introduces direct speech. In (7) *like* acts to downplay (or 'mitigate') the force of an assertion. In (8) *like* may have no other purpose than to fill a pause.

Glossary

adjective: a word like *tall, wet,* or *exciting,* that tells you about the qualities of a person or thing or event (see **29, 32, 74**)

adverb: a word like *slowly, well, there,* or *now,* which tells you about the circumstances of an event, such as how, where or when it happens (see **74, 80**)

adverb phrase: a group of words that has an **adverb** as its **head**, like *very slowly, so often* (see **78, 80**)

adverbial: a word or group of words that functions like an **adverb** and gives you more information about the circumstances of an event. Adverbials can be **adverb phrases**, like *very slowly,* or **prepositional phrases**, like *in the corner,* or noun phrases, like *yesterday afternoon* (see **80, 81**)

adverbial clause: a subordinate clause that functions like an **adverb**, and supplies circumstantial information, e.g. of time, manner, or purpose, to a sentence (see **76**)

article: the **determiner** *th*e (definite article) or *a/an* (indefinite article) (see **14–17**)

aspect: a **verb** form that expresses the speaker's view of the event described by the verb, such as whether it is in progress, or complete. There are two aspects in English: *progressive* (*continuous*) and *perfect* (see **50–57**)

auxiliary verb: the grammar words *be, do* and *have,* along with the **modal auxiliaries,** that precede the main **verb** in a complex verb phrase to add **aspect, voice** and **modality,** and to perform such operations as question formation and negation (see **37, 41**)

clause: a group of words containing a **verb,** forming the main structure of which sentences are built (see **76, 77**)

cohesion: the way that elements, such as **phrases, clauses** and sentences are connected to form text (see **9**)

complement: a syntactic element that completes the meaning required by another element, typically a **verb.** Also, that part of a **clause**

that gives more information about the **subject**. In *Kim is a plumber*, *a plumber* is the **complement** of the verb *is*. An *object complement* gives more information about the **object**: *They named him <u>Cecil</u>* (see **79**)

complement clause: a subordinate clause that completes the meaning of a **verb, adjective, noun** or **preposition**, as in *I think <u>it will rain</u>. It's hard <u>to tell</u>* (see **76, 88**)

conditional clause: a **clause** that usually starts with *if*, which tells us about possible or hypothetical situations (see **43**)

conjunction: a word like *and, but, so,* that links two **clauses**, or **phrases**, or words (see **76, 98**)

corpus: a collection of naturally-occurring language, stored digitally, and accessible for research purposes (see **3**)

countable noun: a **noun** that has both singular and plural forms, and which can be used with *a/an* and numbers: *a cat, three cats* (see **12, 13**)

determiner: a word, like *the, some, my, many, no,* etc. that belongs to the class of words that can go at the beginning of a **noun phrase**: *<u>the</u> black taxi; <u>my many</u> cats* (see **18, 19, 21**)

discourse: language in use in the form of connected speech or writing (see **9**)

dummy subject: a word like *there* or *it* that fills an otherwise empty **subject** slot: *<u>There</u> was a dragon. <u>It</u> was raining* (see **92, 93**)

end-focus: the principle by which new or important information is placed towards the end of a sentence or clause (see **92–94**)

end-weight: the principle by which long phrases tend to be placed at the end of a sentence or **clause** (see **72, 88**)

finite (verb/clause): a verb that is inflected for **tense**, or a clause that has such a verb (see **75, 76**)

genitive: the form of the noun taking *'s* to indicate possession: *the <u>dog's</u> breakfast* (see **30**)

head: the core word in any **phrase** and the one that specifies what kind of phrase it is, e.g. a **noun phrase:** *the dog's <u>breakfast</u>* (see **11, 78**)

imperative: the uninflected form of the **verb** used to give commands, not normally having a **subject:** <u>Go</u> *away!* (see **75**)

infinitive: the **non-finite** verb form, either on its own (the bare infinitive) as in *you made me <u>love</u> you*, or preceded by *to* (the *to*-infinitive) as in *I want <u>to dance</u>* (see **39, 79**)

inflection: a **suffix** added to **verb** stems, **nouns** or **adjectives**, that has a grammatical meaning, such as the past **tense** *-ed* in *asked* (see **2, 34**)

intransitive verb: a **verb** that does not take an **object:** *The train <u>arrived</u>* (see **77**)

lexical aspect: the way a **verb**'s meaning is understood, e.g. as a state (as in **stative verbs**) or as an activity, and, if an activity, whether one that has duration (*she slept*) or one that happens momentarily (*she shouted*) (see **50**)

modal verb: a type of **auxiliary verb** such as *can, may, should, must,* etc. which is used to express possibility and to make offers, suggestions, commands, etc. (see **44, 58–68**).

modality: the lexical and grammatical means, including **modal verbs,** by which logical and personal meanings are expressed (see **58–68**)

modifier: any word that precedes or follows the **head** of a **phrase** to add an extra layer of meaning: *a <u>red</u> bus; the man <u>in the suit</u>* (see **11, 29, 78**)

non-finite (verb/clause): the form of the verb that is not inflected for tense or person, as in **participles** and **infinitives,** or a clause whose main verb is non-finite (see **38, 76**)

noun: a word like *bus, driver, journey, fare, request,* etc. that can be used after a **determiner** as the **subject** or **object** of a sentence (see **74**)

noun modifier: a **noun** that modifies another noun, as in <u>*business*</u> *hours,* <u>*summer*</u> *term* (see **11, 29**)

noun phrase: a word or group of words consisting of at least a **noun** or a **pronoun** and which functions like a noun: *last night; your old car; I; those big red London buses* (see **11**)

object: a **noun phrase** which refers to what or who is affected by the action described by the **verb**: *I caught **the bus**. I paid **the driver*** (= indirect object) ***the fare*** (= direct object) (see **76, 82, 91**)

particle: an **adverb** or **preposition** that combines with a **verb** to form a **phrasal verb**: *get <u>back</u>, look <u>after</u>* (see **42**)

participle: the forms of the **verb** that take *-ing* (present participle) and *-ed* in regular verbs (past participle) (see **35, 38, 40**)

passive: a **verb** form such as *is made* or *was written* where the **subject** is the person or thing that is affected by the action, as compared to the active (*makes, was writing*) (see **71–73**)

phrasal verb: a **verb** and **particle** combination, which often has idiomatic meaning. For example: *What time did you <u>get back</u>? I <u>take after</u> my mother* (see **42**)

phrase: a word group consisting of a **head** and optional **modifiers** (see **78**)

predicate: the part of the sentence that gives information about the **subject** (see **75**)

preposition: a word, or group of words, like *in, on, behind, in front of,* which can indicate place or time, and is always followed by a **noun phrase**: *<u>in</u> the bedroom, <u>on</u> Monday, <u>out of</u> the window* (see **96**)

prepositional phrase: a **phrase** consisting of a **preposition** plus **noun phrase**: *in the bedroom, on Monday, out of the window* (see **78**)

pronoun: a word like *she, me, it, you,* etc. that can be used in place of a **noun phrase** as **subject** or **object** of a sentence (see **22**)

quantifier: **pronouns** or **determiners** that express quantities: *all, both, lots, some* (see **13, 18**)

quotative: an expression that introduces direct speech: *she <u>said</u> 'Hello'; he<u>'s like</u> 'Hey!'* (see **87, 101**)

relative clause: a **clause** that comes after and modifies a **noun**: *the man who came to dinner* (see **83, 84**)

stative (or state) **verb:** a verb that describes a state rather than an action: *she is at work; it costs $10* (see **50**)

subject: the **noun phrase** that typically comes before the **verb** and tells you who or what is the agent or topic of the clause: *I caught the bus. The bus was crowded.* (see **75, 76, 91**)

subordinate (or dependent) **clause:** a **clause** that cannot stand on its own, such as a **relative clause** or an **adverbial clause** (see **75, 76, 86**)

syntax: the grammatical system concerned with how words combine to form **clauses** and sentences (see **74–76**)

tense: the **verb** form which shows whether the speaker is referring to past, present, or future. In English, technically, there are only two tenses: present (*they go*), and past (*they went*) (see **45–47, 49**)

transitive verb: a **verb** that takes an **object**: *She fed the cat* (see **79**)

uncountable noun: a **noun** which cannot be counted, and which therefore has no plural form and does not follow *a/an* or numbers: *some bread, a lot of noise* (see **12, 18, 19**)

verb: a word or words such as *has, worked, costs, takes off,* that follows the **subject** of a **clause**, and expresses states or processes (see **74, 75**)

voice: the choice of active or **passive** verb phrase (see **71–73**)

zero article: the absence of a **determiner** before a **noun**: *I like Ø ice cream* (see **15, 20**)

Index

Printed in the United States
By Bookmasters